D0373314

COWBOY

COWBOY

*The Ultimate Guide
to Living Like a Great American Icon*

ROCCO WACHMAN
AND
MATT PELLEGRINI

HARPER

NEW YORK · LONDON · TORONTO · SYDNEY

HARPER

"CMT Cowboy U" used with permission by CMT.

COWBOY. Copyright © 2010 by Rocco Wachman and Matt Pellegrini. All rights reserved. Printed in the United States of America. No part of this book may be used or reproduced in any manner whatsoever without written permission except in the case of brief quotations embodied in critical articles and reviews. For information address HarperCollins Publishers, 10 East 53rd Street, New York, NY 10022.

HarperCollins books may be purchased for educational, business, or sales promotional use. For information please write: Special Markets Department, HarperCollins Publishers, 10 East 53rd Street, New York, NY 10022.

FIRST EDITION

Designed by Justin Dodd

Library of Congress Cataloging-in-Publication Data is available upon request.

ISBN 978-0-06-177395-2

10 11 12 13 14   OV/RRD   10 9 8 7 6 5 4 3 2

Rocco:

To Damian, John, and Monica Wachman
for their endless efforts and support;
To Lloyd and Lori Bridwell
for their knowledge, patience, and love;
And to Zach, Jeremiah, Gracie, Abigail, and Hannah.

Matt:

To my dad, who made us tough;
To my mom, who made us dream.

CONTENTS

CONTENTS

FOREWORD

I was six years old and riding atop Pancho, my trusted horse, on the forty-five-thousand-acre ranch where I grew up and where my dad worked as a cowboy. As I rode alongside my dad on the crest of one of the tallest mountains on the spread, I reveled in the beauty of the cowboy world in which I was so fortunate to live—the wondrous hills, the breathtaking valleys, and the peaceful Cuyama River—that is, until a nest full of yellow jackets attacked poor Pancho like a squadron of fighter planes.

In a flash, Pancho was running full speed and bucking better than the best of the broncs at a rodeo. I knew that I had only two choices: hold on and live, or die. Needless to say, I scratched and clawed and grabbed for leather anywhere I could.

Eventually, Pancho escaped, and I managed to stay on his back for one reason and one reason only. Throughout the entire ordeal, I constantly repeated the words my dad had preached to me almost every day of my life: Cowboy up!

When my dad caught up with Pancho and me, and he realized I was okay, his eyes twinkled. He smiled and said, "I'm proud of you, son. You cowboyed up and made a hand."

Hearing those words come from a cowboy like my dad made me the happiest boy on earth.

That story had slipped my mind for many years. Thanks to *Cowboy*, I was given the chance to relive it and remember just how important it is for all of us to cowboy up in life and pay attention to all that the cowboy world can teach us.

The more I read this book, the more it brings to mind hosts of other lessons and values I have learned from cowboys throughout my life as a world champion bull rider, bull riding instructor, actor, writer, and, most important, cowboy.

My grandfather, a rancher in the Texas panhandle, sold off his prized cowpony to pay off a debt, teaching me the importance of keeping a promise even if it means making the ultimate sacrifice. My mother taught me that old-fashioned cowboy cooking can nourish not only the hungriest of bellies but also the most starved of souls. And my dad showed me that a guitar and a story can not only get your toes a-tappin', but set the most restless of minds at ease.

Cowboy is filled with practical instruction, advice, and lessons just like these. And there's no doubt you'll walk away from your experience here with all the tools you'll need to begin your journey toward becoming a real-as-it-gets cowboy.

So, get reading, keep your head full of lofty thoughts, and no matter what the world throws your way, cowboy up. It's the only way to live.

> *Adios,*
> *Gary Leffew, Hall of Fame and*
> *World Champion Bull Rider*

INTRODUCTION

There we were, two strangers from different backgrounds, separated by a generation, standing among the quarter horses, paints, and palominos in the main barn at the Arizona Cowboy College. We were entrenched in a conversation about the topic that had somehow landed us in the same place at the same time: the Great American Cowboy.

As we leaned against the stalls, our hats tipped back and our boots dusty from the pulverized caliche, we traded stories about everything from the highs and lows of raising cattle to the intricacies of building a successful career on the rodeo circuit. We discussed the future of the cowboy way, the Hollywood cowboy stereotype, and the cowboy's impact on the economy. But no matter what topic we covered, we always ended up right where we started: the incomparable cowboy spirit.

We soon found ourselves on horseback under a blazing high-noon sun, weaving through the saguaros, searching for cattle. At our sides were Jezebelle and Piper, two cowdogs, who, like any worthy ranch hands, refused to stay back at headquarters when there were cattle to be worked. As the dogs scoured the terrain, we rode along in silence, looking toward the horizon for answers to the fundamental questions: What is a cowboy, and how do you get to be one in mind, body, and spirit?

Upon returning to the ranch, we enjoyed a fine home-cooked meal and continued our conversation well into the evening and throughout the following day. The subjects ranged from spurs to Charlie Sampson to chuck wagon cooking.

By the end of our time together, we arrived at the same conclusion: Whether we are ranchers, teachers, cooks, stay-at-home parents, or corporate executives, the cowboy plays a role in all of our lives and is as important today as he was some 150 years ago, when he came into being in this country.

We shook hands, cementing a partnership driven by one goal: we would create a book that answered, for us and for the rest of the world, the questions we considered on our desert ride. Our book would be a salute both to the cowboy and to the inner cowboy in all of us.

With this premise in mind, we began our literary cattle drive, all the while delving deeper and deeper into living the cowboy life. We rounded up steers, played our guitars, trained horses, and talked until . . . well, the cows came home. We faced our share of hardships along the way just as our predecessors had on the Chisholm and Goodnight-Loving trails. And like the cowpunchers who'd roamed the open range before us, we knew we had no choice but to push onward.

Amid our share of tragedies and triumphs, we survived the journey. The result is what we hope is an accurate, enriching, and entertaining account of the lifestyle we so cherish.

Your adventure begins with a brief history of how the cowboy came into existence in the United States and why he continues to thrive today. Then we'll load up the trailers and head out to the real ranches of the West, where you'll learn about roping and riding, the roundups and cattle drives, branding calves, and much, much more as you wrangle alongside a working ranch cowboy during his sixteen-hour day. When the work's through, you'll stir the pot with Cookie, the famed chuck wagon cook, who'll dish up a highly prized supper of chicken fried steak, pinto beans, biscuits, peach cobbler, and a host of other tasty morsels, all on the open flame of a campfire. As you savor these culinary delights, you'll lean back against your saddle while the cowboy whets his vocal cords with a shot of whiskey, pulls out his six-string, and sings out a melody that'll make you jump up and glide into a Texas two-step.

Afterward, you'll hear what it's like to ride a wild-as-they-come bucking horse, wrestle a steer, and barrel race at the Super Bowl of the Wild West, the National Finals Rodeo in Las Vegas. And when you nestle down into your bedroll and close your eyes under a starry midnight sky, the cowboy will extend a final courtesy by tipping back his hat and lullabying you to sleep with a tale of times long past.

Along the way you'll discover a lot of things that will come in handy on and off the range, such as how to throw a rope, ride a bull, judge a grade of beef, dance a fast-paced triple-step, play a cowboy song on the guitar, purchase the right kind of hat and boots, cook a scrumptious Dutch oven meal, enhance your management and leadership skills, improve personal relationships, and, most important, incorporate passion into everything you do.

By the time you're done reading, a few of you may decide to pack it up, head west, buy a spread, and raise a herd. Fantastic! We can always use another good hand. And for those of you who decide you're happy where you're at, that's great, too. You don't need to work on a ranch or wear spurs to be a cowboy. What's important is that you walk away from this book with a new perspective, a healthy serving of cowboy skills and lore, and an appreciation for the countless ways in which the cowboy tradition influences and betters your day-to-day life.

Welcome to the wonderful world of the cowboy.

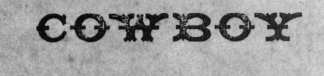

COWBOY

ONE
Cowboy Roots
THE ORIGIN OF THE ICON

The year was 1865 and one of the bloodiest periods in our nation's history, the Civil War, had come to an end. Homes were destroyed, money was short, and jobs were scarce. But strewn among the destruction and loss was one commodity in great supply: cattle, tens of thousands of them dispersed across Texas, New Mexico, and Arizona. These cattle, tough and lean, with horns spanning over six feet in length, had migrated up from Mexico, where the cattle industry was alive and well and had existed for hundreds of years.

 COWBOY TRIVIA
It's a little-known fact that cowboys come from diverse ethnic backgrounds. During the glory days of the American cattle drives, one quarter of the working ranch cowboy population was black, one quarter Mexican, and one half white. Cowboys take pride in the fact that their lifestyle welcomes people from all walks of life.

Businessmen saw in the cattle the opportunity of a lifetime. Bring beef to the people and reap the profits, they thought. Yet, as with most brilliant ideas, there was a catch. The cattle were roaming free across millions of acres of rugged land called open range, where the only boundaries were those that existed in nature. And the main market for

the cattle was thousands of miles away, along the eastern seaboard.

 COWBOY TRIVIA
In 1876 there were fewer than six people per square mile living west of San Antonio, Texas.

The businessmen, who became known as cattlemen, needed a labor force of sizeable proportions to gather the cattle and transport them to the East. As luck would have it, the manpower shortage in the West was met by a surplus in the East, drawn mainly from those whose lives had been consumed by the war. These veterans needed to work. They needed to escape. They needed to survive.

COWBOY TRIVIA
Those who headed west to work cattle were male, typically thirteen to eighteen years old, of European descent, and, on many ranches, required to be single.

The hopeful ventured west, where they signed on with the greatest cow operators of the time. There they were taught the skills needed to work the cattle by vaqueros, Mexican cattle herders who had come to the United States to share their knowledge of the trade.

In Spanish, the word *vaquero* means "cowboy," and those who learned from these Mexican cowboys were known as cowboys themselves. With this simple English translation, the cowboy tradition began.

ROCCO SAYS

If you think that cowboys came only from the lower fringes of society, guess again. Theodore Roosevelt, the twenty-sixth president of the United States, was a Harvard College graduate and a diehard cattleman who not only lived the cowboy life he embraced but also wrote extensively on the subject to preserve its beauty for future generations.

The vaqueros were excellent instructors because they already had a several-hundred-year history of wrangling cattle in environments as tough as, if not tougher than, those they would face north of their border. So they used their experiences to teach their American counterparts how to ride, rope, round up, and brand, along with a multitude of other skills that would not only come in handy on the range, but would also help to ensure their survival in the wilds of the West.

COWBOY LAW

In the Old West, when strangers passed each other on the trail, they never turned around to look at one another after passing. To do so was considered cowardly and an insult if either stranger turned out to be a good man. The same rule applies today.

While the training and work on the home range was demanding for these up-and-coming cowboys, it was nothing compared to their hired task of driving cattle to market. In order to succeed in their jobs, it was necessary for the cow-

Cattle Drives of the 1800s

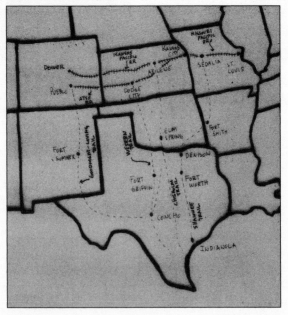

boys to possess fortitude and determination as tough as the hides of the animals they worked.

COWBOY TRIVIA
The Hawaiian cattle industry started in 1793, many years before it did on the mainland.

A cattle drive was one of the most dangerous activities that could be undertaken on the western frontier. Often the cows had to be herded over a thousand miles to the railroads, imposing upon cow, horse, and man a near-death sentence. There were treacherous rivers to cross; snakes, bears, and mountain lions on the prowl; and Indians who would massacre a cow crew and steal their cattle and horses. In modern vernacular, the cowboys would have called the land en route to market "rough country."

COWBOY TRIVIA
Over the years cowboys have answered to many names: cowpoke, cowpuncher, caballero, and cowman, to name a few.

But there was some respite from the struggles of the cattle drive. Most of the time, cowboys could count on a hot meal cooked in an open fire pit behind the chuck wagon that often tasted better and was more generous than what most of the hands ate at home. And every now and again, when they weren't too exhausted, the cowboys would gather around the campfire, where one might recite a verse of poetry or break out his guitar and sing. If the mood was right, a few might even rise from their seats on the ground and break into dance. As simple as these pastimes seemed, they kept the cowboys as happy as they could be in the unforgiving environment of the West.

Despite the almost unbearable ruggedness of the world in which the cowboy lived, the drives succeeded—at least most of them did. However, there was always a price to pay in the form of saddle sores, tuberculosis, tooth decay and infection, broken bones, and of course death. But in the cow-

boy's mind, there was no better life to lead, for it was a calling in which he escaped the horrors of war, saw a land many only dreamed of, and, most of all, determined his own fate.

If you want to get a real taste for what it was like to be a cowboy in the 1860s, you need to visit the National Cowboy and Western Heritage Museum in Oklahoma City, Oklahoma.

By the late 1800s the industry and cities of the East were growing at a rapid pace, and as a result, demand for beef was greater than ever. To meet the increasing demand, eastern businessmen expanded the railroad to reach more territories across the western United States. With railroads now closer to the home range, cowboys no longer had to drive their cattle as far to reach the railheads and get them to the market. In addition, cattlemen increasingly used barbed wire to fence in their herds, decreasing the need for cowboys to patrol vast amounts of land to manage the cattle. Suddenly, the open range was no more.

COWBOY TRIVIA

Barbed wire was invented by Michael Kelly in 1868, and from 1874 to 1884 thousands of patents were issued on variations of barbed wire, although few were ever produced in any significant quantity.

And so, not long after the rise of the cowboy, began his great decline. Some cowboys headed back east. Others stayed in the territories they'd come to think of as home, homesteading small ranches of their own. And some possessed the stubbornness to continue pursuing the lifestyle they had grown to love, roaming freely among ranches in search of work. But even though the twenty-some-year history that marked the pinnacle of the cowboy's historical existence may seem brief, it was forever burned into the minds and culture of this nation, thus defining the cowboy's captivating image.

Believe it or not, today there are still cowboys out there living, working, and playing just as they did in the 1800s. Their gear is newer, and their saddles more comfortable, but they still ride horses and round up cattle. They cook and eat their meals behind a chuck wagon under the open sky. And they strum their guitars and sing songs to nothing but the cows and the tumbleweed.

For these cowboys, the centuries-old traditions they maintain extend well beyond nostalgia. It's a system that's been proven to work time and again. And although it's a lifestyle that may appear well past its prime, it is one that would be virtually, if not foolishly, impossible for the rest of the world to live without.

The cowboy's undying dedication to what he has done, and continues to do, in his world over the course of the past century and a half has elevated him, in the eyes of the non-cowboy world in which most of us live, to iconic status in which he enjoys almost mythical qualities.

 COWBOY TRIVIA
For the past several years, members of the United States Congress have advanced a resolution in support of designating a "National Day of the Cowboy," in honor of the achievements and contributions cowboys have made to American history and society.

Among those qualities are an adventurous soul that finds great joy in facing the unknown, a never-say-quit attitude that overcomes any obstacle, a free spirit that allows him to roam the land wherever he believes destiny leads him, a ruggedness that almost gladly accepts and conquers the hardships life bestows upon him, an unquestionable faith in himself and the men with whom he works and depends on for survival, and an inner strength that allows him to forge ahead when all odds are stacked against him. He is honorable, trustworthy, polite, deliberate, displays etiquette and good manners, and is well dressed and manicured when in public. He is also a romantic by nature, and an enigma to most who do not live in his world. He represents the yin and yang, the good and the bad, depending on the situation at hand. And he is, first and foremost, a gentleman—unless duty obligates him to act otherwise.

In short, the cowboy has sex appeal.

The looks, charm, wit, character, and chivalry all wrapped into one larger-than-life package make him downright irresistible in the eyes of the public. But even these qualities do not adequately describe why the cowboy holds such fascination for us.

COWBOY TRIVIA
John Wayne was posthumously awarded the Congressional Gold Medal for his contribution to preserving and promoting the American West.

When we really think about it, the ultimate allure of the cowboy just might come down to the fact that he *can't* be described in words. Who really knows? More important, who cares? The reality is the cowboy is sexy, and there's no changing that.

COWBOY TRIVIA
Famous Western-themed artist Frederic Remington painted the majority of his creations in Manhattan.

Nevertheless, his attributes and actions are what caused people around the world to develop a love affair with the

Annie Bianco-Ellett

American cowboy. As a result, with the advent of media technology, cowboys began to creep into pop culture. Radio programs such as *The Lone Ranger* focused on cowboy adventures. An entire genre of motion pictures, "Westerns," centered on the cowboy, and from them sprang the likes of Gene Autry, Will Rogers, and John Wayne. Novelists such as Louis L'Amour devoted their careers to portraying the life and times of the cowboy for the public. Many such works were eventually adapted into scripts and placed on the big screen.

REAL-DEAL PROFILE

It's quite possible that the old saw "looks can be deceiving" might never ring truer than when a person sets his eyes upon Annie Bianco-Ellett.

Sure, she's got a smile that could charm the rattle off a rattlesnake, but that doesn't mean she's not one tough cowboy. If you find that hard to believe, then try this on for size: Annie is the only woman ever to win a world championship in the highly competitive sport of cowboy mounted shooting. When you consider the thousands of men and women out there vying for that same title, that's no accomplishment to be taken lightly.

But Annie knows that part of the value in doing what she does comes from the satisfaction she gets in being able to pass on her knowledge to others, which she does in courses at her ranch in Arizona. And that's what makes her a champion in the eyes of every cowboy.

Broadway caught wind of the popularity and allure of the cowboy with the Rodgers and Hammerstein production of *Oklahoma!* And then there's music—everything from renditions of "Home on the Range" to performances by greats such as Hank Williams, Tex Ritter, and Garth Brooks.

We could continue on for days discussing the American cowboy's importance to society and pop culture, but it would mean nothing if you didn't understand this: The cowboy's allure is part and parcel of a long history of not only enduring the hardships life has thrown his way, but also conquering them. Without this aspect, the cowboy wouldn't matter. Fortunately for us, the cowboy and the spirit he personifies are alive and well for all of us to appreciate, enjoy, and embrace.

But enough talkin'.

It's time to start learning about and living the cowboy life, since that's the only way to truly appreciate the cowboy's treasured past and, more important, become a cowboy yourself.

Now, go gather your horse and saddle up. We've got work to do.

TWO

The Twenty-first-Century Cowboy

ALL IN A DAY'S WORK

When it comes right down to it, being a real-life cowboy starts and pretty much ends with one thing: ranching. The term *ranching* gets tossed around pretty loosely these days, so we're going to give you a definition that's as straightforward as it gets. Ranching is all about raising cattle—from insemination to birth to the time they're sold at market. In theory it's simple. But when it comes to running a ranching operation, the strategy and management necessary to turn a profit are anything but elementary, and they certainly aren't for the faint of heart. There are horses and cattle, branding and calving, the commodities market, conservation, and stewardship. The smallest details can mean the difference between life and death and riches and poverty.

Don't think for one second that a rancher can't function outside his rural environment. Sure, his vocabulary and actions may be a bit different than those of his counterparts in the city, but successful ranchers will surprise even the most astute urbanite with their knowledge of current events, business, and world affairs; their ability to adapt to their surroundings; and their thirst for the company of people who live in a world far from their own.

COWBOY LAW

Never ask a rancher how many head of cattle he owns. That's like asking a person how much money he has in the bank.

THE HERD

As you can probably imagine, ranching begins with one thing: the herd. For our purposes, a herd is a group of cattle you call your own. Sometimes you buy the herd, sometimes you inherit the herd, and sometimes you are plain lucky and find the cattle along the way. The important thing to remember is that the herd needs to perpetuate and grow. It's the only way to keep a ranch afloat. To make

sure the herd continues to thrive year in, year out, you need a female cow, or a heifer, and a male cow, or a bull. But you just don't put a bunch of heifers out in the pasture with a bunch of bulls. There's a definite method to the madness.

ROCCO SAYS

When dining on steak, cowboys go for bone-in rib eyes and New York strips, always prime or choice grades, that are fried in a cast-iron skillet. The bone imparts added flavor to the end product, and the skillet allows the beef to bathe in its delicious juices while cooking—both adding tremendously to the cowboy's eating experience.

To ensure that enough calves will be born each year, the rancher has to maintain a certain ratio of bulls to heifers.

The exact number depends on the ranch, water, and a host of other variables that are so fluid in nature that an optimal number is virtually impossible to calculate. Rainfall might be less than required. The price of feed might skyrocket. Calves might fall prey to disease and predators such as mountain lions. Some will be stillborn, some will die after birth, and others will lose their mothers and die. The list is endless. And as a result, the rancher has no choice but to do his best to predict the unpredictable. The rancher's job, therefore, is to place his bets where they are most likely to pay off.

This calculation is even more critical when one considers that the main goal of the rancher is to obtain the highest price for his beef when he sells it at auction or to the market. And the goal within that goal is to obtain what's called a "premium" on the beef. A premium is paid to ranchers who produce beef with a higher "dressed-out" percentage, or a higher percentage of useable beef. The earning of a premium label is what separates real-deal ranchers from those who raise a few cows to supplement their income at Christmastime.

RANCHING MUST-READS

Ranch Life and the Hunting Trail, by Theodore Roosevelt and Frederic Remington; *Lazy B: Growing Up on a Cattle Ranch in the American Southwest*, by Sandra Day O'Connor and H. Alan Day

To earn that premium, the rancher has to do everything he can to make sure that the best bulls mate with the best heifers. Volumes have been written on how to do this, so we're not going to recap them in full here. But suffice it to say it's a delicate art that's complicated many times over by hard science. The important thing to remember is that genetics plays a big role in creating the premium cuts of beef you purchase at your local super-market.

It's largely believed that the best beef comes from raising European breeds of cattle, such as Hereford and Angus. The yield, or the percentage of the cow that is beef versus bone and organs, and the quality of the marbling, or fat content, of the European breeds is the highest, producing the best beef.

 RANCHING TRIVIA
The U.S. Department of Agriculture operates a voluntary beef-grading program that uses two factors to judge the quality of the beef: marbling, or fat content, at the twelfth rib section, and the age of the animal at slaughter. After judging, the beef receives one of the following eight "grades": prime, choice, select, standard, commercial, utility, cutter, or canner.

COWBOY TRIVIA
Dogie is a term used by cowboys to denote a mother-less calf.

But if this chapter so far has got you thinking that ranchers are all about the bottom line, it's time to set things straight. Sure, the rancher has to pay the phone and electric companies just like the rest of us, but when it comes down to it, he loves what he does, or he wouldn't do it. The pay borders on minimum wage—even less in some cases, when you factor in the reality that most ranchers who do it the old-fashioned way work six to six and a half days per week, and many days may last upward of sixteen hours, depending on what needs to be accomplished.

Bear in mind, too, that the rancher is dealing with living creatures, not boxes on a storeroom shelf. For that reason, he has no choice but to put his all into making sure that his herd is healthy. If this means working 'round the clock fixing a well to make sure that the cattle have water, the rancher will do it. If it means feeding a newborn calf by hand from a bottle all hours of the night, he'll do it. If it means helping out a neighbor whose cattle have broken through a fence at eleven o'clock at night, he'll hitch up his trailer, load his horse, come to his neighbor's aid, and return home at sunup, just in time to go right back to work on his own spread. That's just the way the rancher is.

ROCCO SAYS

Cowboys don't need extreme sports. Every day of a cowboy's life is an extreme sport—from riding bucking horses to fending off mountain lions to corralling ornery steers.

Many ranchers in Texas prefer to breed a Texas longhorn with a Hereford, Angus, or Black Baldy heifer when the heifer is breeding for the first time. The reason is that it's statistically more likely that the heifer will proceed through the birthing process with fewer complications, which imparts less stress on the calf and makes for a greater likelihood of survival down the road when external factors come into play.

ROCCO SAYS

It's not a stretch to claim that every businessman in America would do himself justice to spend some time with a rancher learning the ins and outs of managing a herd, which requires expertise in forecasting, financing, employee relations, government regulations, environmental issues, and much more—all managed on a bubblegum budget.

But, back to the ranch.

Let's assume that life goes according to plan, and the rancher gets his prize bull to mate with that award-winning heifer. Nine months later a calf is born. Most often this takes place out on the range, where the cattle graze. It's natural birthing at its essence. No ranchers, no veterinarians, and no interference. And if you think that when a rancher sees one of his heifers throw out a calf he feels any less blessed than when one of his children are born, you'll have a line of cowboys from Corpus Christi to Kalispell who'll tell you otherwise.

WHERE TO LEARN HOW TO BE A WORKING RANCH COWBOY

Arizona Cowboy College, Scottsdale, Arizona

Once that calf is on the ground and standing, the rancher lets the calf—which many cowboys call a baby—roam free on the range, where it'll feed off its mother's—or, in cowboy lingo, momma's—milk and start growing. During that process, the calf does exactly what it is supposed to be doing: gaining upward of two to three pounds per day.

But in the midst of this, or any other distractions that might come his way, the rancher never forgets about his cows—all of them. Never. He's thinking about them while he sleeps, checking in on them while he's awake, and planning the eventual roundup while he's eating dinner.

THE ROUNDUP

Anyone who's ever watched a Western on television or the big screen has heard of a roundup. It's the means by which a rancher gathers his herd and transports them to a designated location where certain activities can be performed. Traditional ranchers do it today in exactly the same manner as the cattlemen did it back in the 1800s.

The first thing a rancher does is put a call into his neighbors to see if they are available to help. Ranchers who work the range the way cowboys did some 150 years ago can't make a living with many, if any, full-time employees. The numbers just don't work. So when more help is needed, the rancher calls up his neighbors, who are usually ranchers or ranch managers themselves. If they aren't available or if he requires more help, the rancher has to find some day workers, or cowboys who travel from ranch to ranch as necessity demands.

Many ranchers affectionately name their cattle, either as groups or individually. For example, one rancher calls a group of his cows the "nuns," because of their white faces and surrounding black hair. Another names his bulls after head coaches at the University of Texas.

Ed Hanks

REAL-DEAL PROFILE

Ed Hanks is the boss of the Triangle M Ranch in Arizona's Prescott Valley. Ed's been in the ranching business his whole life, from growing up on the family spread in Dacona, Colorado, to running horses out of Estes Park, to working cattle down in the desert Southwest. But that's not what makes Ed a cowboy.

Ed loves the land, people, and livestock he works with. For, without those things, what he does would have no value. So how does Ed show his love? In a rather unconventional way.

When tensions mount, Ed is renowned for hollering out a forceful "Goddamnit!" followed by the first name of any hand or animal whose attention he desires. And as much as many a hand has a tale to tell of being on the receiving end of a *goddamnit* from the boss, Ed's curse has become in no uncertain terms both a direct order and a term of endearment. Cowboys who ride alongside Ed can only hope to hear *goddamnit* bawled in their direction.

It's about making sure that the horses, cows, dogs, and people are safe, no matter what's going on. It's about love. It's about being a cowboy.

The rancher and his help, or hands, as they're commonly known, will number from one or two to more than a dozen, depending on how many calves need to be gathered and how much terrain has to be covered. At a rancher's request, they'll saddle up their horses and head out onto the range to find the cows.

In vegetation-sparse areas like the Arizona Desert, cowboys travel in single file line until they get to the point where they know the cattle are near. The reason for crossing the terrain in this manner is that the grass on the range is what makes the cattle grow. If everyone took a different course across the land, they would trample valuable grass and feed for the cattle. In the process, the rancher would be shooting himself in the

pocketbook, and in no time at all
he'd be out of business.

ROCCO SAYS
The services of a good hand never fall out of demand on a
working cattle ranch.

It's critical to keep at the forefront of your mind that ranching is, first
and foremost, a business. The minute the rancher forgets that is the
moment he loses it all. For this very reason, every single action taken
on the ranch, from choosing which horse to ride for the day to decid-
ing how many head to graze, is thought out and reworked again and
again. The rancher is speculating not only with his entire investment
each and every day, but with his livelihood. Because of this, it's no
exaggeration to say that one poor choice by a rancher—whether cutting his herd too thin or selling off a stud in the
corral—could send a rancher looking
for the nearest bankruptcy attorney.

Mind you, the cattle aren't just hanging out in one big
group having a party. Nope, they're scattered across the
countryside. You'll find some of them alone, many times in
groups of three or four, and every now and then in groups of
ten or twenty or more. The hands' job is to hunt them down,
bring them together, and escort them back to the corral in
one group.

FORMATION FOR GATHERING COWS
(IF YOU'VE GOT THE HANDS TO DO IT!)

The boss of the crew—the ranch owner or manager—takes the "point"
position at the front of the herd so he can direct the movement of the
group. A few cowboys will ride on each side of the herd in what's called

the "flank" position. Lastly, some of the cowboys ride, or "drag," in a position behind the herd, where they can keep the herd moving along. The idea is for each cowboy to keep a close watch over the area he's patrolling. In doing so, the hands maintain the integrity of the herd and can follow at a moment's notice any orders the boss calls out.

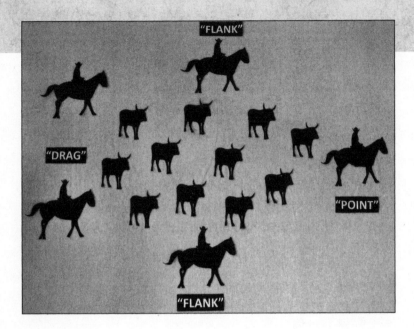

When cowboys are searching for cows, they call out, "Up!" but using two syllables: "Uh-up!" Calling out to the cattle serves two purposes. First, it gets the cattle moving. Second, it helps locate unseen cattle in "rough country," or land extremely thick with brush. In such areas, the cattle can't be seen, but experience tells the cowboy that cattle may be tucked inside clusters of trees or bushes. By calling out, the cowboy surprises the cattle, and they move, allowing the cowboy to spot them, drive them out of the dense foliage, and escort them home.

COWBOY TRIVIA

"Absentee" ranchers are folks who buy a spread, put some cattle on it, live somewhere else, and let their cattle graze freely for a year or so, after which the owners return to round up their cattle for market. The problem with absentee ranching is that the cattle become accustomed to the absence of human beings, so they run away at the mere sight of them. Not only does it make the roundup many times more difficult, but when the cattle dart for the hills at the sight of humans, their adrenaline kicks in, causing them to sweat and burn off the valuable marbled beef they were put in the pasture to produce in the first place. Absentee ranching is a lose-lose situation for all—the rancher, the cattle, and the eventual consumer.

ROCCO SAYS

In order for the rancher to achieve his goals—personal, business, or otherwise—he must, first and foremost, love the process he is undertaking, for he faces continual frustration on the range: too little rain, endless fences in need of repair, flat tires when transportation is required most . . . and the list goes on. It is in traveling down the trail and overcoming any and all hardships that come his way that the rancher finds the most joy, and success, in what he is doing.

RANCHING TRIVIA

A remuda is a group of horses from which a cowboy selects his workhorse for the day.

And by escort, we mean walk—and a slow walk at that. Sorry, folks, but this ain't like you might see in the movies, where the cowboys and their cows storm across the frontier. Moving cattle fast only stresses them, which burns off weight and toughens the meat. That's the last thing a cowboy wants to do.

COWBOY LAW

Causing stress or injury to cattle is the easiest way for a hand to get kicked off a ranch.

If everything goes according to the boss's wishes and the cattle behave like good little cows are supposed to, it's a great start to the day. But like people, not all cattle will do what they are supposed to do all the time, and some run off in a different direction altogether.

ROCCO SAYS

One of the highest compliments a cowboy can receive is to be considered a good "hand" by the ranch boss.

You might be thinking, why doesn't the cowboy pull out his rope, throw it around the straying cow's neck, and bring it back to the herd? The answer is clear: If you have to use your rope, you've done something wrong. If cows run off, either one of the hands wasn't doing his job and let the herd get away from him, or the cowboy who came across cows with behavior disorders didn't use his riding skills to bring those cows back to the herd. The result is unnecessary hardship on the horse and rider, which exponentially increases the chance of injury to both. Committing such a mistake is costly in every respect, and the only way around it is to avoid it completely. It's one of those situations where the less pressure a cowboy puts on the cattle, the more receptive the cows will be to following the cowboy's wishes.

COWBOY TRIVIA

It's been estimated that a cow can run as fast as thirty-five miles per hour.

Once those smart cowboys have successfully driven the pack of momma and baby cows into the corral, they close the gate. Now comes the tough part.

THE COW-WORKING

In order for cowboys to do their work, they have to separate, or "cut," the babies from their mommas. This is where a good horse can mean the difference between a short day and a long lunch or a long day and only a slight possibility of supper.

ROCCO SAYS

If you think human mothers are protective, give them a pair of horns, an extra eight hundred to one thousand pounds, and set them free in the wild, and you'll get a taste of what it's like to attempt to put a momma cow in one pen and her baby in another.

But there's one thing that makes the cowboy's job a hell of a lot easier.

Enter the cutting horse.

A cutting horse is not a specific breed of horse, but rather one that possesses an innate sense of how to cut a cow out of a herd. The horses receive a specific type of training to perform this kind of work. When you see a good cutting horse in action, the cowboy does little directing, because the horse knows where to go. It's almost as if the cowboy and horse are on autopilot. That's not to say it's an easy job. To the contrary, it's a job usually reserved for the best of the best cowboys and horses, because the time and effort expended in cutting cattle is directly proportional to the skill of the men and animals doing it.

Think of cow cutting this way. You're standing in the middle of a corral and there are twelve hundred eyes staring back at you. The four-legged bodies attached to those eyes have only one purpose: to stick together. That's the definition of safety in the wild. Then the boss calls out to you that he wants you to get one pair of eyes out of the lot. Yeah, you heard right—one cow out of six hundred. You can bet your hide that your success or failure depends on the quality of the horse beneath your saddle.

Most male cowboys worth the land they work will tell you that female cowboys have a stronger knack for working with the herd. And those same tough and gruff cowboys will tell you that they attribute this to an inherently motherly instinct that none of us men will ever possess without major reconstructive surgery— and even that's a long shot. But it's true.
And real cowboys aren't afraid to
put the women in charge.

Elaine Pawlowski

REAL-DEAL PROFILE

Underneath Elaine Pawlowski's prettier-than-a-Rocky-Mountain-wildflower hide is a woman who's as tough as any man riding the range. It's who she is and, maybe in part, who she's had to become. Dealing with cowboys is no easy task whether you're a man, woman, horse, cow, or otherwise. And becoming one of them is just shy of impossible.

Elaine is the jigger boss at the Arizona Cowboy College in Scottsdale, Arizona. A jigger boss's most important duty is to ensure the health and welfare of the horses on the ranch. That obligation comes above all else—including taking care of herself. A person doesn't get appointed to the position of jigger boss. It's one that the wrangler with the largest cojones takes as his own. Elaine did just that when she arrived in town, and there's not a cowboy out there who's going to take that role from her as long as she has anything to say about it.

That mentality goes a long way toward preserving the spirit that defined the cowboy 150 years ago and still defines him today.

★ COWBOY LAW

Don't ever call a female ranch hand a cowgirl. Out on the range, everyone is a cowboy, no matter what their gender. The only thing that matters is if someone can do the job.

Once the ranch hands have cut the babies from their mommas, they dismount and break out the branding irons.

 ## COWBOY TRIVIA

With an estimated four to six million cattle roaming the open range, of which tens of thousands were owned by numerous cow operations, the cattlemen back in the mid-1800s needed a way to identify their cattle. So the ranchers resorted to fire and iron and designed a brand that would tell each rancher which cattle were his.

Cattle brands are no less serious business today than when the ranchers began using them in the 1860s. Just like a trademark, brands are registered, in either the county or state in which the ranch resides. When a rancher wants to register a new brand, notice is provided to all other ranchers so that they may approve the brand. Approval in this sense refers to whether or not a rancher believes a new brand too closely resembles his own brand. If it does, and the objecting rancher makes a successful case to the governing body, the brand will not be approved.

 COWBOY TRIVIA

"Riding for the brand" is an old expression used to designate which ranch, or outfit, a cowboy works for and connotes an overwhelming sense of pride and uncompromising devotion.

THE BRANDING

How the rancher gets his registered brand on the calves is a feat unto itself. It is not a one-man operation. When a rancher is going to brand some calves, he needs to do a whole lot more than just place a hot iron on their sides. A branding also usually includes earmarking, inoculation, and castration. It may seem like these activities don't exactly fit together, but like most things a rancher does, efficiency is the key. There's no reason for the rancher to spend one day branding and then another day inoculating, and so on. Getting it all done at once is easier on the crew and the cattle.

The branding crew is broken down into several smaller crews. There are ropers, flankers, branders, inoculation administrators, and the cowboys who perform the castration. Here's how it all fits together:

The ropers are on horseback, and they ride into the herd of calves, swing their lariats, and throw a perfect loop around a calf. Sometimes it's around the neck and sometimes around the leg. Then the roper leads the calf over to the flankers. The flankers are the cowboys who do the dirty work. They have to get that calf on the ground. The calves, which generally weigh in the vicinity of 150 pounds, don't want anything to do with the cowboys, so they resist. The flanker's job, therefore, is to grab that calf and place it on its side on the ground without causing any injury to it. Once that's done, one of the flankers holds the calf's head in place while another holds onto its hind legs so that the cowboys working on the calf won't get kicked.

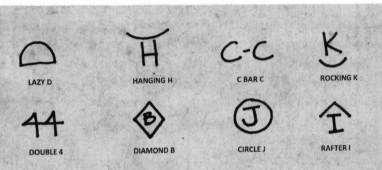

LAZY D

HANGING H

C BAR C

ROCKING K

DOUBLE 4

DIAMOND B

CIRCLE J

RAFTER I

HOW TO READ A CATTLE BRAND

Brands can contain letters, numbers, symbols, and shapes and are read from top to bottom, left to right, and outside to inside.

THE BEST-EVER RANCHING MOVIES

Lonesome Dove, starring Robert Duvall and Tommy Lee Jones (1989); *The Cowboys*, starring John Wayne (1972); *Red River*, starring John Wayne (1948).

Another cowboy then comes in and earmarks the calf. To do this, the cowboy uses either a knife or a special cutting tool that resembles a pair of pliers to nip off a portion of the calf's ear. It's kind of like a giant ear piercing. The reason ranchers do this is so that when the calf is standing out in a pasture, the rancher can determine which cattle are his simply by looking at the earmark on the calf, which may take the form of a semicircle, notch, or many other variations.

While the ear is being notched, one ranch hand steps over to the calf and inserts a needle through its thick hide, injecting a vaccine that will help the calf fend off disease. It's the same principle as the booster shots you received as a kid.

Then the flanker who is manning the hind end looks between the calf's legs to determine if it is male or female, after which he calls out "heifer!" or "bull!" If it's a heifer, the ranch hands wait for the branding iron. If it's a bull, one of the cowboys comes over with a knife and makes a small incision in the calf's scrotum, then reaches a finger inside and pulls the testicles outside the skin. The cowboy then cuts off the testicles, after which the bull is called a steer.

Somewhere during this time, one of the hands removes a white-hot branding iron from a fire and applies it to the side of the calf. When branding is complete, the calf is let loose. The cowboy picks himself off the ground, beats the layers of dust from his chaps, and gears up for the next one.

With a good crew, all of this—incredibly—takes only fifteen to twenty seconds per calf. Once again, the idea is to ensure that all two- and four-legged creatures remain safe and healthy. If the boss can sit back at the end of the day without an injury to anyone or anything, that's a fine day on the ranch.

You might be wondering if all this hurts the calves. Keep in mind that a cow's hide is five times thicker than human skin. It can take much more of a beating than our human skin can. As for the castration, we liken it to circumcision. Yeah, there's certainly some pain involved, but it's over in a flash, and the calves forget about it in no time at all. From our experience, it certainly seems that the worst part for the calves is being

held down. It doesn't hurt them, but it goes against their nature, so it's something they'd rather avoid. Unfortunately, it's something that has to be done for their own welfare.

BACK TO THE PASTURE

Once all the calves have gone through this process, the cowboys mount up and push the cattle back out into the pasture, which out west can consist of anything from a hundred acres or less to more than ten thousand acres, depending on the spread. Once back on the range, the cattle graze on the natural vegetation present all around them.

The number of cattle that can graze on a ranch is largely a matter of the terrain. In Arizona's Prescott Valley, the allotment is roughly one cow per eighty acres per year. Over in greener Shackelford County, Texas, the allotment is closer to twenty-five acres per cow per year. The allotment is controlled by the government, which bases its determination on vegetation levels and a host of other factors in the area.

ROCCO SAYS

If you want to find your way into a rancher's heart, ask him about water. It's arguably the most valuable commodity on the range. In fact, most ranchers spend a great deal of their days making sure that their cattle have water, and they pass a great many nights praying for rain.

Dining almost nonstop on rangeland vegetation during the several months following the branding process, the babies grow by leaps and bounds. Then the day comes for the ranchers to wean the babies from their mommas, or separate them into different pastures. The time to do so is when the babies have developed to the point of living on their own without their momma's milk or guidance. The age at which the rancher performs this task depends on many factors, from the state of the beef market to the price of fuel to the health of the herd. Once on their own, the calves will fend for themselves until they reach a weight of around four to five hundred pounds, which occurs about five to six months after birth.

TO MARKET

As we mention earlier, ranching is a business. Excelling in this industry takes years of experience to master. Most old-timers on the ranch will tell you that they never stop learning or trying to learn. The smallest things can bring a successful career to an abrupt halt. Also, like most businesses, after you've been at it a while, certain aspects of it appear formulaic. But upon taking a closer look you'll quickly discover that within that seemingly routine work is an endless list of variables.

One of the most complex decisions a rancher makes is when to ship his cattle to market. The market can mean two things: selling cattle at auction or shipping them to a feedlot to pack on more weight. Selling cattle at auction is exactly what it sounds like. You transport your cattle to auction, and then buyers bid on your cattle and they are sold to the highest bidder.

The auction can be the perfect place for the smaller rancher to sell off his herd if he does not have the resources to ship his cattle to a feedlot. The downside to selling at auction is that the rancher may not receive the best price for his beef if he normally produces cattle that are highly likely to return prime and choice cuts of meat. However, if the rancher has developed a personal relationship with the auctioneer, and if the auctioneer knows that a particular rancher consistently produces high-grade beef, then the auctioneer might take the initiative to start the bidding at a higher price, thus earning the rancher the premium on his beef that we discuss earlier. The purchaser of the beef is a often a feedlot, which will then spend from a few months to a year putting additional weight on the cattle before they're sold to a meat-packer.

ROCCO SAYS

As with any business venture, the personal relationships a cowboy nurtures on and off the ranch are key factors in determining his long-term success.

The idea behind this strategy, which is highly utilized in sparsely vegetated country, is for the rancher to avoid using up his feed on calves. If the calves were allowed to eat all the vegetation on his land, there would not be enough left for the bulls and mommas to thrive and create new calves. As a result, the rancher would not be able to produce enough cattle to stay in business.

The rancher's other choice is to ship his cattle to a feed-lot directly, instead of selling them. In this scenario, the rancher still owns his cattle, but he pays the feedlot to "fatten up" his animals, that is, increase the weight of the beef until it reaches the 1,100- to 1,300-pound range. This is the weight at which meat-packers will purchase the beef. This is an expensive decision to make for the rancher, because he has to front the cost of feed, veterinary care, and any other incidental costs that may arise before the cattle are sold to the packers.

Ranchers who habitually produce prime cuts of beef will usually make more money by retaining ownership of their cattle and sending them to a feedlot. Instead of being paid for a four- or five-hundred-pound cow, the rancher will eventually sell off a thirteen-hundred-pound animal. Yes, the cost to do this is higher, but if done right, and if the cattle produce the expected prime cuts, the economic benefit to the rancher will outweigh any downside.

When the rancher raises and sells off his cattle in this manner, there is only one way to tell if he has actually produced the best cuts of beef. He has to wait until after the cow has been slaughtered and the meat is hanging on a refrigerated railcar. At this point a meat inspector walks in and grades the beef. If the rancher has done his job, the inspector will give the beef a high grade and the rancher will then be paid for his beef based upon that grade. A few days later, that same beef will be sitting in your local grocery store, luring you to take it home, grill it up, and do it culinary justice.

One out of ten Americans works in an agriculture-related occupation. Even more astonishing is the fact that the loss of one agriculture-related job in this country causes the loss of four nonagricultural jobs.

Consider how many feed plants, veterinarians, pickup truck and horse trailer manufacturers, railroad workers, beef processing plant employees, commodities and futures traders, food wholesalers, grocery stores, and department stores, to name a few, are required so that you can have leather soles on your wingtips or a succulent rib eye on your grill? The numbers are mind-boggling.

But the rancher's value resides not only in beef and leather. What would an artist do without the finest horsehair paintbrushes? What would women do without the horse fat that has been rendered down and become part of lipstick? What about soap? What about drugs, such as Premarin, which is derived from pregnant mare's urine and is used in the treatment of menopause and osteoporosis? Never thought of those things, did you?

Like most things in life, those that require the most effort generate the best results. Producing cattle is no exception. It's a tough life, and to one degree or another it's a crapshoot every day. But to a cowboy, it's the heart of who he is—and worth every minute of the effort. Even more, it's the basis from which all other facets of the cowboy's life extend—from cooking to dancing to wrestling steers. Because of that, all cowboys have ranchers to thank for their continuing way of life.

In fact, we all do. Ranchers provide us with food, demonstrate a work ethic that is difficult to match, and show us how to successfully run a business that is statistically doomed to fail. They are an invaluable link to history, a prime of example of love and devotion to a belief in a cause, and they thrive on passing their knowledge along to others. They are some of the last true free spirits to roam the great American frontier and serve as an inspirational role model for anyone and everyone who dares to tread down the trail less traveled, no matter where it may lead.

THREE

Cowboy Gear

THE ART OF LOOKING THE PART AND MASTERING THE TOOLS OF THE TRADE

When you picture a cowboy in your mind, what do you see? A ten-gallon hat and a faded long-sleeve shirt? A belt buckle the size of a satellite dish and boots worn in the toe? Or perhaps a dusty bandana tied around the neck and a pair of smoking six-shooters?

Well, the truth is the cowboy sees the same picture in his mind. It's just that his perspective is likely to be a bit different than that of the non-cowboy.

You see, the cowboy's gear is as much a part of his life as his horse or dog, and although the hats, shirts, and rifles may look prettier than a Montana sunrise, the cowboy doesn't wear and use them just to look a certain way. Precisely the opposite is true. When the cowboy's at work, he couldn't care less what he looks like. What's important is that his gear serves a purpose no matter what he is doing.

The usefulness of a particular article of clothing or piece of equipment is as much a function of its qualities and characteristics as it is the cowboy's ability to select the right equipment for the job at hand. That's exactly what we want you to learn here, so let's get started.

To explain these essentials, we're going to take a top-down approach. No, this isn't some Ivy League dissertation about trickle-down economics or anything of the sort that we're gonna holler in your direction. Here, by "top-down," we mean we're starting with the cowboy's hat.

THE HAT

Though the cowboy hat immediately paints the picture of a lone man perched atop a bay horse on a ridge overlooking the Sonoran Desert, or a singer bellowing out a tune on the stage of the local saloon, the cowboy hat is much more than an accoutrement in the cowpuncher's attire. The cowboy hat is a tool, just like a helmet is to the football player or a mask is to the welder, and it is multidimensional in purpose. Some of its uses are obvious, such as shading the cowboy's eyes from the glaring midday sun and directing rain on to the back of his slicker rather than down the neck of his shirt; while others are not, such as using the hat as a battering ram to plow through brush as dense as canvas when pushing cattle through rough country. This versatility is the root of the universal appeal of this style of hat within the cowboy community.

But not just any cowboy hat will do.

ROCCO SAYS

Black hats are not reserved for the bad guys, and lighter-colored hats not for the good. The truth is that many cowboys wear black hats in the colder months because the color more easily absorbs heat from the sun. And in the hotter months, many cowboys don a lighter silverbelly-colored hat because it more readily reflects the heat from the sun.

The best hats are made of 100 percent beaver fur, although few people can afford these, as they can cost as much as a small automobile—and we're not exaggerating. For those of us who have to work for a living and can't afford a second mortgage to pay off the loan on a hat, we purchase hats made from a combination of beaver and rabbit fur. The quality of the hat is measured by the ratio of beaver fur to rabbit fur contained within the "felt," and the ratio is designated by an X, with a higher X factor correlating to a higher beaver fur content. Practically speaking, the higher the ratio of beaver fur to rabbit fur, the better the quality of the hat and the longer it will last.

In the old days, a 10X beaver hat meant that the hat contained 100 percent beaver fur. However, times have changed, and the X factor and the relative percentage of beaver fur have fluctuated among hat manufacturers. For example, a 100X label on one hat may mean the same as a 1000X hat on another, and neither or both may contain 100 percent beaver fur. We know it makes no sense, but that's the way it is, because the X ratio has never been standardized in the hat making industry. The point is you have to read your labels and understand the standards the given manufacturer uses to determine its products' X factor.

COWBOY LAW

Never touch a man's hat while it is on his head. It's a matter of respect, and a golden rule among cowboys to be broken under no circumstances.

Beyond its construction, a cowboy hat says a lot about the man wearing it. Depending on the size and shape of the crown and brim, a hat can sometimes tell you where the cowboy is from and what his job is on the ranch. For the cowboy who depends on his intuitive ability for sur-

J.W. Brooks

vival, this comes in rather handy when you come face-to-face with a stranger, for a man's hat just might give you a good idea of whom you're dealing with, which can help you make the best of a bad situation or make a good situation great.

REAL-DEAL PROFILE

If you think a hat is just a hat, then you need to pay a visit to custom hatter J.W. Brooks in Cave Creek, Arizona. Although J.W. uses many of the same techniques and tools as other hatmakers, he remains one step ahead of the rest because he understands that a hat is not just something to cover the head. Rather, it's part of the essence of who a cowboy is and what he represents.

Not only does this attention to detail produce an ear-to-ear grin when J.W.'s customers set their eyes upon the finished product, but it plays a major role in ensuring that the cowboy and his hat never go out of style.

Although we could go on for pages on the subject of the cowboy hat, our discussion really comes down to this—the cowboy hat is one of those seemingly simple articles of clothing whose value is incomparable for the man wearing it and whose uses are limited only by the far reaches of the imagination. It just might be the most important article of clothing that, for the real-deal cowboy, will never lose its value on the ranch, on the range, or on Rodeo Drive.

THE WILD RAG

Moving down, we come to the wild rag, or the bandana tied around the cowboy's neck. This is one area where the fashionably conservative cowboys may take a ride on the flashy side by choosing a color or pattern that is much more flamboyant than the rest of their attire. It's one of the few aspects of a cowboy's persona whereby an outsider might be able to gain a glimpse beneath the cowboy's tough exterior and into the substance of who he is.

TOP-NOTCH COWBOY CLOTHING MEGA STORES
Boot Barn; Sheplers

COWBOY TRIVIA

A true wild rag is composed of 100 percent silk, because of silk's strength and insulating qualities, and is worn wrapped twice around the neck and tucked into the front of the cowboy's shirt.

The cowboy's wild rag is not worn just for flash. It can be used as a mask to keep dust out of the cowboy's lungs or, in winter, placed over the mouth to buffer the bitter cold the cowboy faces in places such as Wyoming and Montana. The cowboy can also yank it off his neck to wipe his face on a sweltering summer day or use it to clean and wrap a wound. It's a piece of equipment that many cowboys consider price- less, and it's only an arm's length away when they need it.

THE SHIRT

Just south of the wild rag is the shirt. There are two kinds of shirts in the cowboy's world. There are work shirts and there are dress shirts. Many cowboys prefer denim work shirts because they can take a beating on the range and come back for more the following day. Others choose lighter-weight cotton because it's a tad bit cooler in warmer climates and, depending on the thickness of the fabric, it might be just as tough as denim. Yet, no matter their shirts' composition, most cowboys desire those with long sleeves, to protect their skin from the sun and the cuts and abrasions that await them on the range. More important, real-deal cowboys require their shirts to have two chest pockets: one for their cattle logbook, or the journal in which they keep track of their livestock, and the other for whatever else they might need to bring along.

ROCCO SAYS

Minimalism is key when it comes to choosing your clothing for a day of work on horseback. It's simply a matter of safety, since fewer articles of clothing lessen the chances of getting yourself snagged on a branch, horn, or saddle.

WHERE TO BUY THE PRETTIEST DRESS SHIRTS AROUND
Rockmount Ranch Wear, Denver, Colorado

As for dress shirts, we're in a different world altogether there. When they're not on the range, many cowboys prefer to wear nicer versions of their work shirts. However, some cowboys prefer to wear what's known as a Western-cut shirt. From a distance the overall shape of a Western-cut shirt is just like that of any other long-sleeve shirt, but when you get up close you realize that the back is scalloped across along the shoulder blades, and in many cases the shirt uses snap buttons, often made of pearl. The decorative aspect provided by the pearl snaps is often accentuated by artistic embroidery elsewhere on the shirt, depicting anything from cattle to hats to palm trees. There's no doubt these shirts will catch your eye and set you on a search to find a store where you can get your hands on one, or two, or maybe even a dozen! And once you've got 'em you'll be looking for the nearest saloon or dance hall to show them off.

THE BELT

Dropping down to the belt . . . Yes, the belt. We'd bet that when most people picture cowboys, in the back of their minds they envision men who walk around wearing belts with buckles the size of hubcaps. There's no question that

Pat Brantley

many cowboys do, when the time and place are right, but the real-deal ranch cowboys shy away from wearing belts while working.

REAL-DEAL PROFILE

Pat Brantley of Burkburnett, Texas, is a Texan through and through. That's no title to be taken lightly, because part of being an honest-to-goodness Texan means being a cowboy and doing what you can to make sure the cowboy way of life continues.

Pat best shows his devotion to the cowboy way of life through his craft: leatherworking. For nearly five decades, he's spent virtually all his free time designing, cutting, tooling, and sewing leather in his workshop, where he has produced some of the finest-quality leather goods west of the Atlantic Ocean.

Whether it's belts, wallets, pillows, or anything else, Pat's products are highly prized for one reason and one reason only: he puts his cowboy spirit into every piece he makes.

For Pat, it's not about the money. No, he does it for a reason much greater: to carry on a centuries-old tradition that is as much a part of the cowboy lifestyle as working cows.

It's because of cowboys like Pat that the Great American Cowboy has not been forgotten.

WHERE TO BUY A NICE-AS-THEY-COME BELT BUCKLE

Montana Silversmiths, Columbus, Montana

The reason? Safety concerns. When a cowboy is out working rough country, there are many things that his belt could get hooked on that could land him in the hospital. For example, if the cowboy's horse starts to buck, his belt could snag on the saddle horn and result in a serious predicament. Or, when he has to make speedy work of barreling his way through trees while trying to catch up with an unruly steer, he might catch his belt on a branch and get jerked from his horse. And, possibly worst of all, when he is working in tight quarters with cattle that still have their horns, the last thing the cowboy wants is for a cow to slip a horn under his belt and yank him from his horse, taking him on one hell of a ride—most likely to the nearest emergency room.

The moral of the story is wear your big belt buckle when harm is not staring you down—like back in the barn or at the dance hall. We can't afford to lose a good cowboy just because he wore his belt when he wasn't supposed to.

JEANS

Now it's time to hit below the belt. Unlike some of the other articles of clothing we've discussed, there's nothing special about the jeans the cowboy wears. He likes them tough and rugged, just like he is, so that they can withstand the hell he's no doubt going to put them through. Beyond that there's not much to be said.

 COWBOY TRIVIA
Many Professional Rodeo Cowboy Association cowboys wear Wranglers for a reason. Whereas most jeans have a thick seam on the inside of the leg, Wrangler designed its jeans with a thin seam, so they would be more comfortable to wear for a cowboy in the saddle. Wrangler was so devoted to providing quality jeans to the cowboy that it spent years of research and development on the product. On the thirteenth try, it got it right, and the Wrangler jean has remained that way ever since.

However, it's likely you'll notice that different generations of cowboys wear different brands of jeans. The old-timers tend to wear Levi's; the next generation, Wranglers; and the younger cowpunchers, whatever the latest brand to make it into the market. This isn't a universal rule, but it's an observation that happens to be accurate more often than not. Just keep your eyes peeled next time you're around some cowpokes and take note of who's wearing what.

That's about all we can tell you on the subject. It's really a matter of comfort, cost, and durability. Simple as that.

CHAPS AND CHINKS

Many cowboys who work rough country don't depend solely on their jeans to protect their legs. Most wear either chaps (pronounced "shaps") or chinks.

This is the perfect opportunity to let you in on another secret about cowboys. Cowboys are bastardizers. They bastardize this and they bastardize that—and that's no insult to cowpunchers. Cowboys young and old have a tendency to take a perfectly fine word and change, or bastardize, it so either it's shorter or it sounds better in the cowboy's ear.

Back in the day, the cowboy listened to the vaqueros speak in their native tongue, and because the cowboy either couldn't understand his Mexican counterparts or didn't care to, he changed the vaqueros' words to suit his needs. For example, *buckaroo*, the word so many people use to describe a young cowboy, is actually a bastardized form of the Spanish word *vaquero*. Why are we telling you this now? Because *chaps* is another such bastardization; it's a shortened version of the Spanish word *chaparreras*.

 COWBOY TRIVIA
Chaps are secured to the body behind the back with a thin latigo, or strip of leather, so that if the chaps get caught on something they will rip away from the body, thereby helping the cowboy avoid serious injury.

Chaps are pieces of leather that run from the beltline to the boots and cover the legs, much like a second pair of jeans worn over the first pair, to protect the cowboy from brush and weather. Chaps, or "leggings," in cowboy jargon, are made in a variety of shapes and sizes. Some fit loose and are shaped like a bat's wings and are called batwing chaps. Then there are the slender "shotgun" chaps, which are worn close to the leg, almost like a second skin, and zip closed from top to bottom. In the colder and snowier climates of the North, cowboys wear "woolies," or chaps covered in wool or buffalo hair.

As with everything the cowboy does, the type of chaps he wears depends on what he is doing. However, there are times when personal style comes into play. This most often occurs on the rodeo circuit, where roughstock riders don chaps of many different colors—from natural rawhide to vibrant turquoises to everything in between—with varying lengths of fringe and with or without "conchos," silver decorative discs that adorn the leather. But for the most part, usefulness is the main consideration in determining which type of chaps are worn.

The other leg-covering option for the cowboy is chinks, which are essentially chaps that have been cut off approximately four inches below the knee. Some cowboys prefer these because they are less confining and offer the cowboy a bit more mobility in carrying out his work. More often than not, chinks are chosen over chaps by Southwestern cowboys, because the reduced amount of leather makes them much cooler in the one-hundred-plus-degree heat. But as with some of the cowboy's other gear, whether he wears chinks or chaps is most often a matter of personal preference.

BOOTS

Next to the cowboy hat, cowboy boots are arguably the second most definable article of clothing a cowboy wears. Real-deal cowboys prefer boots made of leather rather than the exotic varieties made of snakeskin or alligator hide. Show up on a ranch with something other than leather and you're going to be looking at one hell of a day being the object of an endless array of jokes. Save yourself the grief. Wear leather.

TWO OF OUR FAVORITE BOOTMAKERS
Ariat; Justin Boots

Some boots have low, flat heels, while others have larger, angled heels. The shape and size of the heel are key because a properly sized heel prevents the foot from slipping through the stirrups during a ride, which goes a long way toward removing one ingredient in the cowboy's endless list of recipes for disaster.

The angle of the heel plays a role as well, as cowboy boots are designed so that if the horse the cowboy is riding comes to an abrupt halt with its weight shifting toward its hindquarters and its torso almost dragging the ground, the angled heel of the cowboy's boot will allow the cowboy's feet to slide along the ground rather than get hung up.

Another important feature of the boot is its height. Boots generally are made in two heights—those that rise just higher than mid-shin and those that reach all the way up to the knee. The height of the boot is important because most of the time the cowboy is not hanging out on nicely manicured lawns. To the contrary, he often finds himself ankle deep in . . . um, well, let's just say manure. For that reason it helps to have boots that will prevent muck, water, and anything else from leaking into the boot and irritating the cowboy's feet. And because of the thick leather from which boots are constructed, they do a darn good job of protecting the leg from jabbing objects such as barbed wire, thorns, and rattlesnake fangs.

Beyond boots' material, height, and the size and shape of the heel, the choice of what boot to wear is an individual one, and most often a matter of what feels right. The key to finding a pair of boots that suits you is twofold: knowing your needs and trying on a lot of boots. Do those two things and your feet will be thanking you for many days to come.

Our top-down attire analysis doesn't end with the boot, though. We've got one more indispensible item that requires discussion.

SPURS

Now you might think that cowboys like to walk around with these steel contraptions on their heels just to look cool. If so, you're dead wrong. They've got a purpose just like everything else in the cowboy's world.

WHERE TO BUY SPURS

Garcia Bit and Spur Company, at the J.M Capriola Company, Elko, Nevada

The spur is composed of four parts: the spur strap; the heel band, or yoke; the neck, or shank; and the rowel. The spur strap is a piece of leather of varying widths that is attached to the spur, wraps around the upper part of the cowboy boot, and secures the spur to the boot. The heel band, or yoke, is a U-shaped piece of metal that wraps around the heel of the cowboy boot and keeps the spur in place. The neck, or shank, is a narrow metal extension that juts out behind the boot. And the rowel is the star-shaped piece of metal that spins like a wheel at the end of the spur shaft.

Rowels come in many shapes and sizes. Many vaqueros use rowels that look like giant snowflakes, sometimes several inches in diameter. Most American cowboys today use rowels that are about an inch in diameter and are rounded off so they won't injure the horse.

So how do spurs work? When a cowboy steers his horse, he uses his voice, body, hands, legs, and feet to direct the horse to do what he needs him to do: walk, trot, lope, turn, or stop. Although a skilled rider needs nothing more than his own body to accomplish these tasks, spurs allow the cowboy to be more precise in his instructions, which makes life easier for horse and cowboy alike.

Contrary to popular belief, the cowboy does not jam the spurs into the side of the horse. This would hurt the horse, and that goes against everything the cowboy believes. Rather, he uses subtle movements with his spurs to cue, or direct, the horse to move as desired.

Keep in mind that someone doesn't just strap on spurs from day one. Cowboys look at it this way: If you aren't completely comfortable with your horse, and you can't control it without spurs, then spurs aren't going to do you a damn bit of good. Exactly the opposite is true. If you aren't ready to wear the spurs, but you decide to strap them on anyway, do us a favor and call an ambulance before you saddle up, because you're sure as hell going to need it.

In a word we're telling you that you're going to wreck. Not fall off, not get bucked. Wreck. Why do cowboys call it a wreck? Because when a cowboy gets thrown from a horse, the only word that can come even close to accurately describing the monstrosity that happens is *wreck*. It's short. It's definitive. And it can kill you. So don't be dumber than a rotten fence post. Leave the spurs to the experts until you're ready for them.

ROPE

There are two more irreplacable performance aids that deserve mention. The first has a name that, like *vaquero* and *chaparreras*, has been bastardized by the cowboy. It's known as the lariat, or rope. The word *lariat* is derived from *la reata*, the Spanish word for rope.

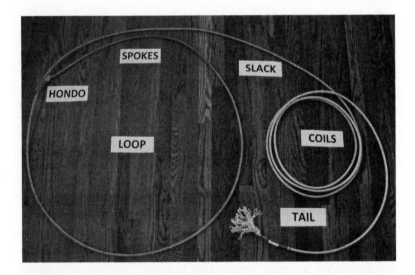

 COWBOY TRIVIA

There are six parts to a lariat: the tail, the coils, the slack, the spokes, the hondo, and the loop. The position and use of each play a vital role in lassoing an animal or other object.

Most cowboys carry attached to their saddles a type of lariat called a ranch rope, which typically runs from forty to sixty feet in length, much longer than the thirty to thirty-five-foot ropes used in rodeos. The difference in length between ranch and rodeo ropes is a function of the task to be performed. Rodeo cowboys need a rope built for speed, and the shorter rope provides them with this luxury. Ranch cowboys need a rope that is more versatile. One day it may be needed to pull a steer from a mud bog, and the next, to rig up a temporary corral for the cowboy's horse. The extra length in the ranch rope allows a cowboy to do this.

TOP ROPE BRANDS

Cactus Ropes, Equibrand Classic Ropes

We don't want you making a fool of yourself when you find yourself talking it up with a real-deal cowboy, so we're going to correct a potentially major error before you make it. You've probably heard a cowboy's rope called a lasso. That's not correct. Lasso is the verb, the act of throwing the rope. It's not the rope. You lasso something with a lariat. You don't use a lasso to lasso. Knowing and using the right terminology will get you one step closer to becoming a cowboy yourself, and it's a surefire route to being accepted by other cowboys.

The material from which the lariat is, and used to be, made is largely dependent on the region from where the cowboy came. Back in the early days, the vaqueros wove their own lariats from rawhide, as they believed the ropes made in this manner were stronger and performed better. Meanwhile, the cowboys of European descent wove theirs from cotton and called them "sea-gos," because they resembled the "sea-going" ropes used by their sailing ancestors. And across the Pacific Ocean, the paniolos, or Hawaiian cowboys, made their lariats out of palm fronds. In many respects, it was a matter of both tradition and what raw materials were available.

Today, some cowboys still weave their own lariats in the same way as their predecessors, but many use ropes made of synthetic material, which theoretically can handle more abuse and last longer. It's really a personal choice, although price does factor in, as handwoven ropes cost many times more than their synthetic counterparts.

That said, save up your money and buy the best rope you can afford. Trust us. The money you spend will be worthwhile when you find yourself in a predicament that only a rope can bail you out of.

FIREARMS

There's one other category of equipment no self-respecting cowboy could live without, and that's his firearms. Although they play nowhere near as vital a role in the cowboy's life as they did over a century ago, firearms are still as much a part of his world as his horse and his pickup truck.

TOP-TIER FIREARM MANUFACTURERS
Sturm Ruger and Co., Inc.; Winchester Repeating Arms Company

Back in the day, a cowboy needed his "six-gun," or his revolver, rifle, and shotgun as much for protection from other men as he did from mountain lions. Though cowboys today certainly know they'll never have to use a pistol on another man, they also know full well that they still need their firearms for protection from the perils of nature.

In much of the rough country where cowboys work today, there are still plenty of predators out there that threaten not only the cowboy, but also his horse, dog, and cattle. There's no question that the cowboy loves his natural surroundings,

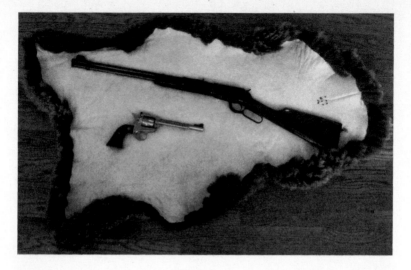

but there's also no question that he has to be prepared for the worst—even though he prays day and night that the worst will never occur. Carrying a firearm and, more important, knowing how to use it is part of that preparation. And even though a cowboy may be armed with a pistol, rifle, or shotgun, his greatest hope is that his firearm never leaves its holster.

But the twenty-first-century cowboy does not rely on his firearms only for protection. They also play an integral role in his leisure activities. Many cowboys participate in target shooting as a hobby. As a result of the popularity of this activity, cowboy shooting competitions have evolved in which a competitor shoots various targets using his pistol, rifle, and shotgun while on the ground or on horseback in much the same way an Old West cowboy would have had to shoot it out with cattle rustlers and the like in the 1800s.

WHERE TO LEARN TO SHOOT LIKE A COWBOY

Annie Bianco-Ellett's Outlaw Annie Bootcamp, Cave Creek, Arizona

Although shooting off hundreds of rounds of ammunition can be awful taxing on the cowboy's pocketbook, it's a recreational activity that cowboys across America enjoy. But even more so, the cowboy is carrying on a tradition that is as much a part of his history as Charles Goodnight and his chuck wagon.

Well, there you have it folks. The cowboy and his gear. These few items serve the cowboy well both on and off the trail, and they will do the same for you whether you're moving cows up near the Big Horns or heading for dinner in Chicago's Loop. So look up your local cowboy outfitter and get yourself well suited up and equipped for the rest of your education, because there's still a lot of work to be done. Just do us a favor and make sure we take you for a real-deal cowboy when we see you. That will be our greatest reward.

FOUR
The Cowboy's Companions
HORSES AND OTHER FOUR-LEGGED OR -WHEELED THINGS

As a surgeon requires his star nurse in the operating room or a judge demands his studious clerk in his courtroom, there's no way you'll ever catch a cowboy doing his job without his most trusted sidekicks right there with him on the wide open range. They are his offense and his defense. They are his board of directors, joint chiefs of staff, his counsel, co-workers, friends, and sometimes those who call his bluff. They are with him through the toughest of journeys and the happiest of victories. And they are so much a part of his life that the cowboy just couldn't live without them.

Let's start with the greatest all-terrain vehicle ever invented: the horse.

ROCCO SAYS
There are only two kinds of horses: those that have spooked and those that will.

Historians say that about five thousand years ago the horse was used for agricultural purposes. Then, around thirty-five hundred years ago, someone came up with the bright idea of riding one of these creatures. And when we further examine history, we see that it has been over only the last one hundred or so years that the horse hasn't been as important in our lives. We have the automobile to thank for that. But don't worry, even with cars congesting our roads, the horse has not yet fallen by the wayside.

ROCCO SAYS

The ultimate goal of every cowboy is to be considered what the Mexican cowboys call a caballero, or a horseman. Achieving this designation entails an absolute mastery of horses and horsemanship, and is reserved for only the best of the best.

Although horses may not be used for daily transportation down the I-95 freeway or powering conveyor belts at Ford Motor Company, the nine million horses and three million horse aficionados, and the forty-five-billion-dollar industry of which they are a part, are as alive and well as they were centuries ago in cowboy country.

ROCCO SAYS

If you want to understand what a horse is thinking, watch his head. If it's tilted downward or straight ahead, the horse is at ease. But if his head is cocked upward, the horse is alert and preparing to go on the offensive or defensive.

To a working cowboy, the horse's importance cannot be overstated. His horse leads him on to the range in the morning, helps him as he performs his daily chores, and carries him back home when the workday's through. A cowboy selects his horse based upon one premise and one premise only: Is it the right horse for the job?

Although choosing a horse may seem like a simple task, it's anything but. In fact, it literally takes a lifetime for a cowboy to begin to understand all the nuances that factor into making such a decision. The best way to describe it is to equate the cowboy's selection of a horse to the way in which a manager chooses an employee in the work setting.

THE MAGAZINE TO READ TO LEARN HOW TO RIDE A HORSE LIKE A COWBOY

Western Horseman

Some employees are patient, some strong, some attentive to commands, whereas others are timid or nonresponsive. A cowboy who is effective at his job takes such characteristics into account when calculating which horse he'll use for the day.

On an easy day, one consisting of checking fences for damage or riding the line to secure open gates, the cowboy will select a younger, less-experienced horse. On a hard day, one that will involve gathering wild cows on some remote rock ledge, the cowboy will choose a horse who has seen it all and done it all. This horse, the one taking on such a hard task, must have the disposition of a Navy SEAL, the heart of a lion, and the agility of a mountain goat.

ROCCO SAYS

Horses are rear-wheel-drive creatures, meaning that they derive all their power from their hindquarters. This trait is extremely valuable for the working ranch cowboy, because it allows him to change his horse's direction in a fraction of a second. For this reason, the horse breed of choice for the cowboy is the American quarter horse, which displays this quality better than any other.

The process of selecting a horse is best explained in the cowboy's own words: We ride the horse's brain. The cowboy understands that a horse's intelligence is the single most important factor to getting a job done efficiently and effectively in the safest manner possible.

Horses have an acute sense of touch. For example, a horse can pinpoint a fly anywhere on its body and can twitch the exact muscle fiber that resides directly below where the fly has landed.

However, it's vital to keep in mind that even though these animals are extremely helpful to their owners, are as personable as Labrador retrievers, and love to be around other living creatures, they are unpredictable by nature. How so? It comes down to the horse's ability to comprehend and assimilate many stimuli at one time.

HOW TO GREET A HORSE

The proper way to approach a horse is just like horses approach one another in the wild. First, nonchalantly walk toward the horse, never looking it directly in the eye. When you are close enough, place your head by the horse's shoulder, as if smelling its scent. Then move your head forward, toward the horse's nose, to let it smell you. Follow these instructions, and you'll have yourself a friend in no time flat.

ROCCO SAYS
Treat a good horse and a not-so-good horse exactly the same.

There's no question that horses focus quite keenly on the job at hand, but if some outside stimulus enters the picture, look out. If it sees a flower that doesn't look right, the horse might spook. If a cowboy spits at the wrong time, the horse might spook. If it forgets you're standing beside him, a horse might spook. The list is endless. And because of its natural inability to handle such situations, the horse might just cause you to wreck. It's not because it doesn't like you, but rather because it's experiencing information overload and its brain can't process all the information in a logical—and safe—manner.

THE DEFINITIVE ORGANIZATION FOR THE COWBOY'S HORSE
The American Quarter Horse Association

HORSE TRIVIA
All horses celebrate their birthdays on January 1.

So what does the cowboy do about it? His options are limited, because Mother Nature is a force more powerful than he will ever be. But there are two courses of action he can take to minimize the chances of experiencing the virtually inevitable.

ROCCO SAYS
The best method for training horses is the "wet blanket" method: training a horse while riding it, during which the horse will sweat, making for a wet blanket between the horse's back and the saddle.

First, the cowboy conditions the horse from the time it is born and in its early years to be less jittery. He does this by sacking out, or touching and handling, the horse and introducing it to the different situations it will encounter down the line when it starts working. This labor-intensive conditioning plants seeds in the horse's brain so that when the same or a similar scenario presents itself in a work setting, the horse will be less prone to buck or rear or throw its rider.

Second, once the horse is old enough to ride, generally after two years, the rider keeps his eyes, ears, and intuition on full alert when working with the horse, to avoid placing it in a predicament in which it might go loco and head for the hills. The good cowboy will not take this responsibility lightly, because he is not only protecting himself and his horse, he is also protecting the cowboys, horses, dogs, and cows who ride beside him. The cowboy knows that putting the time and effort into maintaining a safe environment for his horse will repay him many lifetimes over when accidents are hiding just around the bend.

ROCCO SAYS

The fastest way to train a horse is to take your time doing it.

We could easily write an encyclopedia on horses—and many people have—but our goal is to stress the fact that the cowboy couldn't do his job without this fine animal underneath him. For that reason, the horse is almost considered kin to the working rancher.

GROOMING

Just like with his kin, the cowboy makes sure that his horse is well dressed and groomed.

Believe it or not, the cowboy doesn't groom his horse to make it look pretty. The cowboy brushes his horse because thorns, dirt, nails, and pretty much anything else can get caught in its hair, which can cause injury to the horse when he's out on the trail. If the cowboy were to skip brushing his horse, debris might be trapped between the saddle pad and the horse's back, which could irritate the horse. This might lead to serious health complications for the horse or it might be enough to cause a wreck, and that's the last thing a cowboy needs to worry about on the trail. In this respect, grooming is one area where an ounce of prevention is truly worth a hundred pounds of cure.

TACK

Just as the cowboy requires certain attire and gear to perform his job, so does his horse. The horse-specific equipment upon which horse and rider depend to make work and play enjoyable and safe is called tack. Once the cowboy brushes his horse and picks foreign objects from its hooves, he centers a saddle pad—a padded piece of cloth or foam, or a combination of the two—on the horse's back. The saddle pad prevents irritation to the horse's hide in the place where the saddle will rest.

ROCCO SAYS

At workday's end, a cowboy's first duty is to care for his horse—even before he cares for himself.

COWBOY LAW

Never touch another man's tack. It's completely unacceptable in the cowboy's world unless you're invited to do so.

When the saddle pad is in place, the cowboy grabs hold of his most valuable possession: his saddle. Back in the heyday of the American cowboy, the saddle was often the only thing a cowboy owned, and he would do whatever he had to do to make sure he held on to it. It was a tragedy in any cowboy's eyes to see another cowboy lose his saddle in a poker game or other mindless undertaking, because without a saddle, a cowboy couldn't ride a horse, and if a cowboy couldn't ride a horse, there was no need for his services.

It takes a long time to break in a saddle just the way a cowboy likes it. It's much like breaking in a new pair of leather shoes. It's not a fun time weathering out the discomfort, but once those shoes fit just the way you want them, they couldn't be more comfortable.

With both hands, the cowboy gently rests the saddle, his prized possession, upon the horse's back far enough toward the horse's neck so that if an imaginary line were drawn from the forward edge of the saddle straight down to the ground, the horse's front leg would be bisected. Then the cowboy cinches up his saddle using leather straps, called latigo, which circle underneath the horse's belly and secure the saddle to the horse.

Cowboys who regularly ride rough country most often

use only one cinch, which resides toward the front of the saddle, just behind the horse's front legs. The reason for this is that the second cinch, which rests rearward and more toward the widest part of the horse's belly, is in just the right spot for getting snagged on branches or cow horns, which can create a dangerous situation. But for those cowboys who don't have to ride through rough country, two cinches work just fine.

ROCCO SAYS

Your horse's behavior is a directly proportional to the number of people watching you ride: the more people watching, the worse the behavior, and vice versa.

The cowboy then slips the bridle and bit, which are most commonly composed of leather and steel, over the horse's head and into its mouth. The bit rests gently in the horse's mouth in the space between its front and back teeth, and is attached to lengths of leather, called headstalls, which run along the sides of the horse's head and connect behind the horse's ears. Then the cowboy attaches to the bit the reins, which are thin lengths of leather the rider holds and uses to steer his horse, and loops them over and across the top of the horse's neck.

Does the bit hurt the horse's mouth? The answer is that it shouldn't if it's used properly. Why? Because it's all in the handler. A cowboy who knows what he's doing can use the harshest of bits and not cause a shred of discomfort to the horse. On the other hand, a rider who doesn't know his backside from a Joshua tree can use the gentlest of bits and cause extreme discomfort to a horse. The moral of the story is: learn, learn, learn, and do so under the supervision of someone who knows what he's doing. Educating yourself goes a long way toward avoiding unnecessary grief down the road.

For the most part, we've just given you a lowdown on all the equipment that horse and rider use on a daily basis to make every ride comfortable and safe. Yet comfort and safety do not end there. There's one last area of vital importance to horse and rider that we need to address: horseshoeing.

HORSESHOEING

First let's introduce you to the two people who attach shoes to a horse's hooves: the farrier and the horseshoer. Many people use these two terms interchangeably, but that's just not correct. It's like using *oral surgeon* and *dentist* to mean the same thing. The two are closely related, but they are not exactly the same.

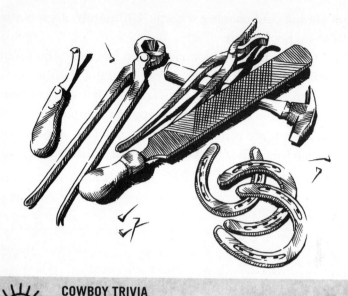

COWBOY TRIVIA

The task of properly shoeing a horse is wholistic in nature. Not only are the horse's hooves taken into account during the process, but also the overall health and anatomy of the animal so that the horse can be fitted for optimum well-being and performance.

A farrier is a person who can take raw bar stock and build his own horseshoes and nails using a forge, hammer, and anvil. He can then "hot shoe" a horse, a process by which the farrier heats a properly sized shoe before securing it to the horse's hoof. It's a method that some cowboys believe produces a better and more comfortable fit for the horse.

A horseshoer, on the other hand, is someone who does *not* make his own shoes or nails. He also "cold shoes" a horse—that is, he does *not* heat the shoe before attaching it to the horse's hoof. With technological advances in horseshoe manufacturing, many cowboys feel that there is no longer a substantial difference in results achieved with regard to hot versus cold shoeing a horse. Ultimately, it's a matter of personal preference.

Practically speaking, a farrier, who has to attend school for certification, has a wider array of skills than a horseshoer. It doesn't mean that the farrier is better at shoeing horses than a horseshoer. That depends completely on the person. It's simply a distinction that must be understood. And it's one that will serve you well when you decide to outfit your herd of horses with shoes.

 COWBOY TRIVIA

The nails used to secure the shoe to the hoof are specially designed. They are flat on one side and beveled on the other. The beveled side always faces the inside of the horse's hoof, to prevent injury. Horseshoers recite a motto to help them remember which side of the nail points inward: "Personality on the inside." What does this mean? When nails are made, the manufacturer imprints a design on the beveled side of the nail. This is called the personality. The personality is said to go on the inside because that's where it resides in a human being.

Every cowboy has to know how to "fix a flat," or repair a shoe that's been lost, because it never fails that at least once in a cowboy's career, a horse will throw a shoe off the side of cliff fifteen miles from ranch headquarters. When this happens, the cowboy doesn't have the luxury of calling AAA, and he's got to rely on what he knows. Because of the remoteness of the territory in which many cowboys work, this is one skill that just might save the cowboy's, and his horse's, life.

THE COWDOG

There's another four-legged critter that follows a cowboy wherever he goes. And he's more of an assistant and best friend. We're talking about the cowdog.

The cowdog is a herding dog in a subcategory known as pastoral dogs, or those bred to work livestock. These dogs have been either trained or bred to herd animals. They come in all shapes and sizes, from scrawny little collies to burly Australian cattle dogs, and like the cutting horse, they possess an uncanny instinct for working cattle.

REAL-DEAL PROFILE

When we think about dependability on the range, two names come to mind: Vaquero Viejo and Jezebelle.

This eleven-year-old Appaloosa horse and six-year-old border collie–American Staffordshire bulldog mix not only understand what it takes to work cattle in some of the roughest country in the West, but they know how to do it well. Sure, a certain portion of that can be attributed to their training, but when it really comes down to it, the devotion, intelligence, determination, and work ethic exhibited by these two animals are tied right in to their internal wiring.

It's the intangible qualities like these that make them the best of companions both on and off the range.

Vaquero Viejo

Jezebelle

Cowdogs generally fit into three more activity-specific categories: they are either headers, heelers, or what we'll call all-around dogs. Headers are the dogs that get in front of the pack of cows to intimidate them, so to speak, into doing what they are supposed to do. Headers have a tendency to crouch low to the ground, like a predator, and use what's called a "strong eye" to show the cows who's boss. Heelers, on the other hand, work the cows from the back and often nip at their heels to get them moving in the right direction. Then there are the all-around cowdogs, or those that can do everything, the jacks-of-all-trades among their fellow cowdogs.

A GREAT SOURCE FOR HERDING DOG INFORMATION

United States Border Collie Club

No matter what the breed, training, or category, a good cowdog plays an integral role in the working ranch cowboy's life. And the cowboy knows it.

All it takes is a command from the cowboy, and a good cowdog will be off to work. And these dogs truly love their jobs. You can see the disappointment on their faces when their master can't bring them along. It's enough to make a cowboy cry.

COWDOG TRIVIA

Just as cowboys don't wear belts when they are working rough country, in order to avoid wrecks, the same goes for cowdogs. They never wear their collars when they are working in areas or situations where the collars could snag and cause injury.

On some ranches a good cowdog can do the work of six cowboys. The dogs can cover so much territory in such a short amount of time that they are worth a fortune to the lucky rancher. Since it's awful tough, if not impossible, for a ranch to keep full-time employees, who can be costly, many ranchers are forced to use dogs to fill these roles. Don't misunderstand us. Cowboys love the company of other cowboys, but looking down at the ground and seeing your favorite cowdog makes the stormiest of situations look like the sunniest. It's a winning combination for cowboy and cowdog.

TRUCKS AND TRAILERS

So now that we've talked about horses and dogs, we've got to fill you in on another of the cowboy's indispensable companions: his pickup truck.

ROCCO SAYS

In this day and age, a cowboy without a pickup truck is like a writer without a computer. Sure, he can still get the job done, but having one makes his life a whole lot easier.

Why is it so important? Well, in some respects it is like his horse, a symbol of freedom, one that allows him to roam the land as he so chooses. In another respect, it is one of the few places where he and his best cowdog can ride the range in search of the day's work without interference from anyone or anything else.

And then there's the more practical side. The pickup truck was made for the working man. And the cowboy is no stranger to work. Yet, as every profession that utilizes the pickup truck has its specialized requirements, so does the cowboy with regard to his rig.

Behind that truck usually comes a trailer, whether it's filled with hay, horses, or cows. Trailers are as diverse as the cowboys who tow them. On one end of the spectrum, you'll see a lot of ranchers with trailers that have more rust on them than solid metal. But for the rancher, if

the trailer still does the job, there's no need to replace it. Rather, he'll do his best to keep it running until it literally falls apart.

At the other end of the spectrum, you'll see horse trailers that cost into the hundreds of thousands of dollars. These include everything from custom mahogany and leather living quarters to horse stalls that are no less extravagant. They've got the shiniest stainless steel on their sides, and they make a huge statement. We're not going to tell you what that statement is, but with everything that we've told you so far, we think you've got a pretty good idea what we think of these.

And then there are the in-between models, which you'll encounter most often. These are the trailers that are sturdy and that do a great job of hauling horses and other livestock. For the most part, they are rather plain, but many cowboys will add a little touch, such as their brand painted on the side, to make it their own. This category of trailer may also have rudimentary living areas, including a bunk and possibly a propane stove. Rodeo cowboys who have to trailer their horses across the country are rather fond of trailers like these because they cut down on hotel costs. These factors make them the most popular of trailers in the cowboy world.

The horse, cowdog, truck, and trailer serve, in no small way, as the cowboy's most trusted allies in the rugged and ever-changing world in which he lives. And no matter where the cowboy travels or what hardships he encounters, he knows that these cherished creatures and things will be there beside him, never stopping until the task at hand is accomplished.

We hope you enjoy the presence of some of these companions in your lives, and if you don't, go out and get yourself some. We assure you that you just might discover some happiness along the way. Plus, we'll have someone new to argue with over the merits of two- versus four-wheel drive.

FIVE
Chuck Wagon Cooking
HUNGER, HOSPITALITY, AND HAPPINESS AROUND THE CAMPFIRE

In life, genius often finds its home in simplicity. And in the cowboy's world, amid the complications of dealing with cows and cowboys, horses and dogs, and trucks and tractors, there may be nothing simpler, yet more ingenius, than a meal cooked over an open fire and served up behind a chuck wagon.

ROCCO SAYS

Cowboys still gather at the chuck wagon for breakfast, lunch, and dinner on a regular basis. This usually occurs when they are working in territory too remote from the ranch headquarters, where they'd normally convene at the cookshack, the indoor version of the chuck wagon

Many of you might believe that the chuck wagon, and the cooking techniques that arose from its use, are a relic of what the cowboy once was. Well, that's not exactly the case. Although they're nowhere near as common as they once were, chuck wagons are still used today on many ranches across the West. However, even where chuck wagons are not used regularly, the hospitality, recipes, and cooking techniques of the early days still remain intact. In this regard, little has changed over the course of the past 150 or so years.

The chuck wagon was invented in 1866 by rancher Charles Goodnight when he and Oliver Loving, his partner in the cattle business, decided to drive their cattle from North Texas to the railhead in Denver, Colorado, where the cattle would then be shipped to market. In order to push their two thousand head up the seven-hundred-mile route, Goodnight and Loving needed a sizeable crew of cowboys.

COWBOY TRIVIA

In the early days, a cowboy wouldn't sign on to work for an outfit on a cattle drive if he didn't approve of its cook or the particular food he prepared.

A sizeable crew meant they would require a lot of equipment and provisions. That's when Goodnight realized he needed something special to haul all that gear in. So he purchased a government-issue wagon and modified it to suit his needs. Most prominently, he designed a box that housed drawers and shelves to store all the essentials a cook might look for in his quest to keep his crew provided with food, which the cowboys called chuck. The box fit on the back of the wagon, sloping downward, and had a feature that was priceless on the trail: the door covering the box dropped down toward the ground and converted into a table from which the cook could work his culinary magic. Some wagons included a "fly," or a canvas tarp suspended over the chuck box, so that the cook would have shelter from the elements.

Although the chuck wagon itself is an amazing mechanical device, much more awe should be reserved for the man who commanded it. The overseer of this most valuable of dining necessities was the infamous chuck wagon cook.

The cook was, and still is, called many names, ranging from Cookie to Coosie to Beanslinger, but those are just those we can mention in public. The cook was also called a few other not-so-nice names, though cowboys found it much safer to use them when the cook was a long way away. Like everything else in the cowboy's world, this not-so-nice name calling was usually for a pretty good reason.

 CHUCK WAGON TRIVIA

The term *cookie* is, in true cowboy fashion, a bastardized form of the Spanish word *cocinero*, which means a cook.

Old Cookie—he was usually older than most of the cattle crew—had a reputation on the ranch and on the cattle drives for being more than a bit ornery. And the use of the word *ornery* is our way of being polite.

Although cowboys were often justified in using colorful names to express their disdain for Cookie, he was even more justified in carrying on the way he sometimes did. On the cattle drives, he served in a multidimensional capacity, acting as father, mother, dentist, doctor, judge, jury, scrivener, and much, much more. After all, when a bunch of young and often hot-headed cowboys got together, there were bound to be at least a few conflicts needing resolution.

ROCCO SAYS

One of Cookie's most important jobs before crawling into his bedroll for the night was to point the tongue of the chuck wagon at the North Star, which served as a makeshift compass so that, come morning, the trail boss knew which way to guide his herd.

When such scuffles sprang up, someone had to make sure that operations proceeded as required. The range boss had neither the time nor the inclination to worry about anything other than the cows, and the cowboys certainly couldn't be trusted to manage themselves. So there was only one person to turn to: Old Cookie.

For his service, Cookie was paid as much as two to three times what the cowboys were paid—and he earned every cent. Rising at 3:00 a.m., he'd build a fire and have breakfast prepared before sunup. After breakfast, he'd distribute biscuits or hard tack (a type of cracker made from water, flour, and salt), and bacon or jerky, which the cowboys could eat during the day if they didn't have time to convene for formal lunches. Then Cookie would clean up camp, pack the wagon, and push ahead to the spot where the cowboys would meet him for dinner. He'd build a fire, cook and serve dinner, clean up, and tend to any of the cowboys' other needs, such as clothes mending, letter writing, or simply lending a shoulder to lean on. Then, somewhere between 10:00 p.m. and 12:00 a.m., he'd retire to his bedroll, just to do it all over again the following day—and the ninety-nine or so after that.

CHUCK WAGON MUST-READS

Forty Years Behind the Lid, by Richard Bolt; *Come an' Get It: The Story of the Old Cowboy Cook*, by Ramon F. Adams

But that wasn't all Cookie did. He also transported all the other equipment the cowboys would need on the cattle drive, which included things such as bedrolls, branding irons, and rifles and ammunition. He was, in essence, the official unofficial director of operations.

As much as Cookie might have been the one cactus into which you didn't want to fall face first, he loved his job and would have it no other way. He was a master of human relationships and an expert in his craft. And the cowboys knew it.

For the cowboys on a several-month-long cattle drive, the chuck wagon was a home away from home, and for many of them, the only home they knew, both on or off the cattle drive. It was the one place where they could lay down their bedrolls at night and know they were safe, where they could share a delicious meal with friends, where they could talk about their joys and sorrows, and where they could sing and dance away what little free time they had. When they needed someone to cut their hair, Cookie was there for them. When they needed someone to pull a rotten tooth, Cookie was there. And when they needed a shoulder to cry on, Cookie was there.

Above all, the cowboys understood that they were blessed with the opportunity to indulge in a daily luxury that few other men had or could ever experience—and they could do all these things under a shining sun and flickering stars in a pristine, wild country that stretched as far as the eye could see. Although it was a life where seemingly endless challenges were encountered at every turn, it was also a life they felt fortunate to lead. In no small way, this grateful attitude was due to the efforts of Cookie and the environment he created around the chuck wagon.

Today, things haven't changed all that much. Cookie can still be the tough-as-rawhide character he has to be, but no matter what his demeanor, his cooking is often some of the best around. Sure, he might have a few modern conveniences now to help him out, but the secret to his success lies in the way he embraces the ingredients, tools, and techniques of the past. It is this knowledge and understanding of the basics that allows him to draw crowds for miles around.

It wouldn't be fair to jump right into the recipes without showing you the basics. In true cowboy fashion, we want you to walk away from this book with a few more skills than you had before you began reading, which means we've got a little explaining to do.

In the old days, the ingredients at Cookie's disposal were basic and minimal, often consisting of nothing more than coffee, flour, salt, a few spices, molasses, beans, potatoes, dried fruits, canned vegetables, and, of course, beef. These were the mainstays from which Cookie had to produce enough of an array of meals to keep the cowboys happy. And a happy cowboy made for happy cows, which in turn made for a happy trail boss. Ultimately, that happiness flowed right on down to the rancher who owned the herd. Now, the word *happy* might not be the perfect descriptor, but in a world where injury or death hides behind every rock, tree, cactus, and mountain, sometimes it can take only a little thing, such as a well-cooked meal, to make a cowboy happy.

 CHUCK WAGON TRIVIA

During those times when Cookie had no hard currency to purchase goods from a general store while he was on the cattle drive, he bought the items he needed on credit. Credit was extended to the brand, or ranch, for which Cookie worked. This was the most widely accepted guarantee for future payment of the debt.

There were certain situations where Cookie had some novel ingredients to incorporate into his repertoire. Occasionally, a cowboy might hunt down wild game or catch some fish while riding the trail, but that was a rarity—and a delicacy—in the day-in, day-out life of the working cowboy. On other occasions, Cookie would trade settlers his beef for their vegetables or eggs. And during those few times when the cattle drive neared a town, Cookie would send some of his cowboys to the general store to buy something different. But these were the exceptions rather than the rule, so most of the time Cookie had to make do with his limited set of ingredients.

COWBOY TRIVIA

In the olden days, line riders, or cowboys who covered territory many miles from a cow camp, or those riding in arid climates, brought along canned tomatoes in place of water. They learned that drinking the tomato juice was better than drinking water to stave off thirst.

You might be wondering how Cookie could make anything beyond a few ordinary meals with such few ingredients. Therein lies his genius. In the world of cooking, the greatest cooks are those who can create the most spectacular meals with only a handful of ingredients. Allow Cookie to get his hands on those raw materials, and you'll be in for a real treat.

But even Cookie will tell you, there's not much he can do without the right equipment. He's not talking about heading into your high-end retailer to buy a knife for two hundred dollars or a salad crisper for fifty. Nope, when Cookie talks about his "equipment," he means one thing: his Dutch oven.

COWBOY TRIVIA

It's been claimed that the Dutch oven received its name from the Dutch traders who peddled housewares, including the cast-iron pot that cowboys grew to love.

The cowboy's Dutch oven is a heavy-duty cast-iron stock pot with a couple of special features. First, a lip encircling the lid allows hot coals to be placed on top of the pot. Second, the pot has three short legs that form a tripod. Both of these features come into play when baking. To bake, the Dutch oven is removed from the fire and placed on a small bed of coals. The three legs provide space under the Dutch oven for the coals, which allows for more even heating during baking. Hot coals are also placed on the lid, to more closely approximate the heat dispersion of a conventional oven. The lip on the lid prevents the coals and ashes from falling into the pot when the lid is opened. With features like these, the Dutch oven allows the cowboy to cook and bake virtually anything that can be cooked or baked in a conventional kitchen oven.

ROCCO SAYS

Eat light when on the trail, because nothing is more uncomfortable than being on horseback with a full stomach.

The second most important item for the chuck wagon cook is wood. You might think that any wood will do, but trying to convince Cookie that he can use any old wood is like telling the rattlesnake that he doesn't need his rattle. Sure, life will go on, but it's just not the same.

When it comes to fueling their fires, most chuck wagon cooks prefer hardwoods, such as mesquite or oak, because of the even heat these woods produce. The secret to a great chuck wagon meal is to burn the wood down to coals and cook over those. Cookie would never, and we mean never, cook over an open flame, because he believes that flames impart inappropriate flavors to the food.

COWBOY LAW

While riding the trail, never fail to bring firewood back to camp, so long as it's not going to prevent you from doing your job.

On trail drives, however, wood wasn't always available. In that case, Cookie generally had two options. The first was to gather the wood and haul it along on the drive, either piling it on a piece of canvas draped underneath the chuck wagon or towing it in the "hooligan," a small wagon towed behind the main chuck wagon. If there was no wood available for hauling, Cookie would often use cow chips, or dried cow manure, to fuel the fire, which burned extremely hot. This wasn't the ideal choice, but it worked well when necessary. We hope you never have to resort to this second method, but if you do, do us a favor and don't tell your guests, because it might be the last time they come around—and we certainly don't want that.

ROCCO SAYS

When out on the range, it goes without saying that the boss eats last. It's a show of the respect a boss has for his crew.

All kidding aside, we're telling you this for a reason, because we want to give you an option when it comes to fixing up some fine chuck wagon–style meals. You can either do it the old-fashioned way and cook over coals, or you can cook the modern way and use the stove and oven in your kitchen. We'll explain both methods in the recipes so that if you get the itch to rough-it like Charles Goodnight, you've got the tools to do it.

WHERE TO SEE AND TASTE REAL-AS-IT-GETS CHUCK WAGON COOKING

Lincoln County Cowboy Symposium, World's Richest Chuckwagon Cook-off, Ruidoso, New Mexico; National Cowboy and Western Heritage Museum Chuck Wagon Gathering, Oklahoma City, Oklahoma

If you're going to cook outside, there are a few simple things you need to know. First, you have to dig yourself a fire pit that is larger than the Dutch oven you will be using. When cooking for large crews, where multiple pots, Dutch ovens, and skillets will be used, a common pit size is four feet long, one and a half feet wide, and one foot deep. This is also the perfect size to accommodate the rack from which some of the pots hang over the fire.

Once you've got your pit ready, you've got to build a fire. If you have access to hardwoods, by all means, use them.

But if you don't, there's a modern convenience that comes in quite handy in this regard, and does a pretty darn good job as well—charcoal briquettes. After you've settled on your fuel, light the fire and kick back with a cold beverage until the wood or the charcoal briquettes burn down to coals that are white hot. This is one area where patience is not only a virtue, but it can also make for a rather enjoyable afternoon with the right libation in hand. Once those coals are ready and nothing remains in your glass but ice, it's time to declare one thing and one thing only: Let the cooking begin!

By now, whether you realize it or not, you're all students of the cowboy curriculum, so it's time to turn you over to Professor Cookie, who'll teach you how to impress family, friends, and strangers alike with some classic recipes from the trail.

COWBOY TRIVIA

Back in the old days, you'd never find a welcome mat at the front door of a cowboy's house. This was a reflection of the fact that everyone—strangers included—was welcome at the cowboy's house, so there was no need to make such an announcement on a doormat.

We do have one warning. Once you start, we'll bet you won't be able to stop until you've perfected your meals. It's one addiction that you'll never have to kick, unless, of course, you're eating a half-dozen chicken fried steaks and a whole pan of peach cobbler every night. And once word gets out that you're the Cookie in your neighborhood, you will never again dine alone.

COFFEE

For the cowboy, all meals on the cattle drive begin with one item: coffee. Up until the end of the Civil War in 1865, coffee beans were sold unroasted, which meant that every morning Cookie would have to roast the beans before he ground and served the coffee. Unfortunately, if one bean burned, it would ruin the whole batch, which happened a lot, through no fault of Cookie's. Thus, cowboys used to drink coffee for its stimulating qualities. Period.

ROCCO SAYS

Cowboys like their coffee strong, more akin to espresso than traditional American-style coffee. Because of their coffee's strength, cowboys developed an array of terms and phrases to describe this most precious of drinks. One cowboy once described the coffee he was drinking as "so thick it would float a horseshoe."

Then came the invention of roasted coffee. The brand of choice was Arbuckle's, which included in every fifty-pound sack of coffee a pouch of peppermint sticks. That seems like an awfully odd choice, but actually it was pure genius. Cookie would use the peppermint sticks as bartering tools. If a cowboy agreed to perform some chores, such as fetching wood, grinding coffee, or washing the dishes, Cookie would reward him with a peppermint stick.

CHUCK WAGON TRIVIA

One of the most common, and well liked, breakfasts on cattle drives of the 1860s to 1880s was warm rice with syrup.

Although a peppermint stick seems like an awful small incentive, you have to remember that sugar and sweets were expensive in the mid- to late 1880s, and thus infrequent indulgences on the ranch and cattle drives. Because of that, when a cowboy who had been on the trail for forty-five days got a hankering for something sweet, the peppermint stick was enough reward to get him to do just about anything. For you ladies reading this, there's an important lesson to be learned: Your cowboy will do just about anything for a little sweetness!

But let's get back to brewing coffee. As you certainly should know by now, everything the cowboy does is based on the premise of making it as simple as possible, and making a damn fine cup of coffee is no exception. We know that most of you are going to turn on your gas or electric stove or automatic drip machine to make your coffee, but we have to tell you that there's something mighty special about fresh coffee pulled off a campfire on a chilly midwinter morning. For some reason that no cowboy will ever be able to explain, the coals and smoke give the coffee a flavor that just can't be matched in a kitchen.

COFFEE
Ingredients
Coffee
Water

Directions
Place the coffee grounds in the bottom of the pot. Fill the pot with water and soak overnight. When ready to make your coffee, place the pot over the fire. When the water comes to a boil, remove the pot from the heat. Add a splash of cold water to settle the coffee grounds to the bottom of the pot.

Some cooks add ground-up eggshell to the coffee, as they believe this produces coffee with greater clarity.

We'll let you decide whether to make your brew in- or out-doors, but whatever you choose, this recipe will result in one of the tastiest cups of coffee you'll ever come across. And you'll never again have to worry about staying awake and alert. Rather, you'll have to find some way to get some much-needed shut-eye.

Don't worry. We're confident that the rest of the food we're cooking here will put enough calories in your belly to lull you to sleep under the midnight stars. But don't go getting any funny ideas about relaxing. We've got a lot of work—and even more eating—to do.

SOURDOUGH

There's no doubt that coffee plays an integral role in the cowboy's existence, but if you really want to get a cowboy excited, all you have to do is mention one word, and he'll be firing off his six-shooters with excitement. The word? *Sourdough*. It's the generic term cowboys use to describe a variety of sourdough-based biscuits, breads, desserts, and other baked goods.

 CHUCK WAGON TRIVIA

The key to keeping a sourdough starter alive is making sure it stays warm. During the early cattle drives, Cookie would place his crock of starter in the sun during the day and tuck it right next to him in his bedroll at night. Needless to say, his nurturing ways with his sourdough became the object of much ribbing from his cowboys.

Sourdough was (and still is) arguably one of the most sought-after items on Cookie's menu. However, the demand was not just for any old sourdough. It had to be good sourdough. No, that's not right. It had to be out-of-this-world good sourdough. And accomplishing that was no easy task. Cookie knew it, too, for with the never-ending stress on the range, one bad day of sourdough might have meant the difference between life and death for old Cookie—and that's no joke. For that reason, if for no other, Cookie did his best to make sure the cowboys were smiling ear to ear after biting into his sourdough.

Many a chuck wagon cook will tell you that the quality of sourdough begins and ends with what's called the starter. Sourdough starter is the basis from which all sourdough recipes are created. Some cowboys claim that their starters are over a hundred years old. Don't get all worked up thinking that you might have been eating something that was made a century ago. It's something much different, and here's what they mean.

SOURDOUGH STARTER
Ingredients

1 cake or package of yeast

4 cups warm water

4 cups flour

2 tablespoons sugar

Directions

Mix the yeast and the water; then stir in the flour and sugar. Set aside for eight or more hours until the starter is light and bubbling.

Some cooks add a potato cut into quarters, which will "feed" the fermenting yeast.

As you use your starter and diminish your supply, always add back in equal parts flour and water equivalent to the portion of starter you have used. For example, if you've use two cups of starter for a recipe, mix back into the starter one cup of flour and one cup of water to keep the starter alive for the next use.

Many decades ago a cook created a sourdough starter. Now, technically, a starter is a living thing because of the yeast, which feeds on the sugars in the starter. This growing yeast is what gives sourdough its sour taste. When Cookie decides to make up some biscuits or bread using the starter, he uses only a portion of the starter to do so. The portion of the starter that remains in the wooden or earthenware crock, or the container in which the starter is stored and which no cook worth his beans would do without, remains alive. Be sure to keep this in mind when you hear someone claim they've got a starter older than your great-great-grandmother. It merely means that Cookie has been keeping the same starter alive over the years and passing it down to the next generation, rather than creating a new starter every time he cooks.

ROCCO SAYS

When cooking with a Dutch oven, experience plays a large part in controlling the heat. So don't shy away from cooking outdoors just because you've burned a few batches of biscuits. The best of the best chuck wagon cooks have done the same thing. The key is to just keep trying, and eventually you'll perfect your technique.

Why in the name of Bodacious the bull would anyone do this? Well, it's the same principle as with certain types of wine. Aging the wine, or in this case the starter, causes higher-quality tastes to find their way into the product and onto your tongue. And when it comes right down to it, all that matters in the end is if you love what you're eating.

BISCUITS

When cowboys think about that decades-old sourdough, one thought comes to mind: biscuits. And just so we're clear, biscuits aren't just for breakfast on the range. They can play an important part in every meal the cowboy eats. There's no question that, at day's end, when Cookie hollered out,

"Come an' get it!" sourdough biscuits would be waiting for the cowboy.

SOURDOUGH BISCUITS
Ingredients

2 cups sourdough starter

2 cups flour

1 teaspoon salt

1 tablespoon sugar

2 tablespoons bacon grease or butter, melted

Directions

Mix all the ingredients except the bacon grease to create a soft dough. Form golf-ball-size pieces. Roll the dough balls in the bacon grease and place them in the Dutch oven. The tighter the biscuits are packed together in the Dutch oven, the higher they will rise. Set the pot aside in a warm place for 10 to 15 minutes to allow the biscuits to rest. Bake at 350 degrees for 30 minutes, or until golden brown.

If cooking outdoors, heat the Dutch oven over coals and follow the recipe as described. Then place a small bed of coals on the ground, and set the Dutch oven over them. Then place approximately two to three times that amount of hot coals on the lid. Bake 20 to 30 minutes, or until golden brown.

Although the best sourdough biscuits can serve as a meal in their own right, there are a few other dishes that can accompany them to make them taste that much better. One such dish is beans.

BEANS

When we say beans, we mean one thing: pinto beans. That's right, plain old ordinary dried-out pinto beans. You might be smiling to yourself, thinking that beans don't make a meal. If you are, just look in the history books or talk to an old-timer cowboy, and you'll discover that pinto beans kept many a man from starving on and off the trail. For heaven's sake, don't underestimate the power of the tiny pinto bean.

RANCH BEANS
Ingredients

4 cups dried pinto beans

2 cups finely chopped onion

4 strips bacon, roughly chopped

Water

Salt

Directions

Soak the dried beans overnight in water. When ready to cook, place the Dutch oven over medium heat. Sauté the bacon until cooked but still soft. Add the onion and sauté until soft. Drain the beans, add them to the pot, and sauté for 10 to 15 minutes. Cover the beans with fresh water until the water is one inch higher than the beans. Simmer uncovered for 4 to 5 hours. Once the beans begin to soften, add salt to taste. Adding salt sooner, along with frequent stirring, will make the beans tough.

Besides fending off starvation, beans still play a vital role in the world of cowboy cooking. Why? There are three main reasons: First, they are inexpensive; second, they store well; and third, and possibly most important, they do a fine job of filling up the cowboy's belly. These three qualities make the bean a natural choice for feeding dozens of hungry cowboys, and for packing along on a several-month-long cattle drive. But even if beans were cumbersome and expensive, they would still be worth eating, because a top-notch pot of beans is a delicacy fit for the king of any cattle operation. If you don't believe us, just fix yourself up a batch, and that will be the end of that argument.

We'll bet the ranch on it!

CHICKEN FRIED STEAK

Now it's time for the main course, and there may be no main course that screams out *cowboy*! better than chicken fried steak. This is one of the most sought-after main courses in all of cowboy cooking, and it shows up in many a camp during the chuck wagon cooking competitions that take place all across the West.

CHICKEN FRIED STEAK
Ingredients

1 egg
Two 6-ounce round steaks, cubed or tenderized
½ cup flour

Oil

Salt

Directions

Beat the egg and dip the steaks in the egg wash. Then dredge them in the flour. Heat ¼ inch of oil in a skillet on the stovetop, or in the Dutch oven over hot coals. Add the floured steaks to the hot oil and fry until golden brown. Salt to taste after removing the steaks from the oil.

If available, render down beef fat and use it in place of cooking oil. Beef fat cooks at a higher temperature, which will produce a crispier steak.

Chicken fried steak is popular for many of the same reasons as beans. For one, beef is plentiful. On the cattle drives in the 1800s, Cookie would slaughter a cow as needed to feed the crew. This worked well for both the rancher and Cookie, because Cookie usually chose a cow that was not going to make it the rest of the way to the railroad. Thus, the rancher did not need to see a good cow go to waste, and Cookie could use that beef to keep the cowboys well fed, and therefore in the right mental, emotional, and physical state to get the work done during the day.

But besides the fact that beef was plentiful, and essentially free, since the cow would have died anyway and not brought in any money at market, beef prepared in this style made for a scrumptious meal, and it kept a cowboy full for many hours. And as you'll discover if you ever find yourself in a cow camp, a full cowboy is one of the best varieties of cowboy there is!

GRAVY

Yet beef is only one half of the key to enjoying a scrumptious chicken fried steak. In some cowboys' opinions, the other half of the equation is equally, if not more, important.

We're talking about gravy. There's no question a chicken fried steak can stand on its own, but as far as the cowboy is concerned,with the right gravy, it's a tough meal to beat.

COWBOY GRAVY
Ingredients

Pan drippings from chicken fried steak

Flour

Milk

Salt

Directions

Add equal amounts of pan drippings and flour to a Dutch oven. Whisk the mixture until smooth in texture, and cook over medium heat until it thickens. Slowly add the milk until desired thickness of gravy is achieved. Season to taste with salt.

Now, gravy on the trail and gravy at the cookshack on the ranch are two different creatures. That's because of one ingredient: milk. When ranch finances were good and the ranch could purchase milk, or if it had its own milking cow, milk was the liquid of choice to create a creamy gravy. However, on the range, hundreds of miles from home and sometimes civilization, milk was nowhere to be found. In that case, Cookie used water as a substitute. You might be wondering if the same texture and quality can be achieved. Well, there's one place to look, and that's with the experts—the cowboys. There are accounts where cowboys back at headquarters eating at the cookshack actually requested that the gravy be made with water rather than milk. Those damn cowboys kept Cookie on his toes as much as Cookie did them. We'll let you decide your preference, but whatever it is, there is one rule you absolutely must follow: Smother that steak with gravy!

You're welcome. We say that because we know you'll be thanking us once one tiny drop of that delicious nectar hits your taste buds. And you'll be thanking us—and Cookie—again when you have enough gravy left over, after gobbling up your chicken fried steak, to sop up and

enjoy with the rest of the sourdough biscuit you've been
saving for the occasion.

DESSERT

By now your belly has to be full, or at least it's aching to be
full. But we can't leave you just like that. No self-respecting
cowboy would depart from the chuck wagon without eating
dessert, and there's no way we'd let you, either.

As we've mentioned, in the 1850s, sugar and sweets were
expensive, which made them a luxury on both the ranch and
the cattle drive. Nevertheless, Cookie knew that satisfying
food was one of the best gifts he could give to the cowboys before they climbed into their bedrolls at night. And though biscuits, beans, beef, and gravy work just fine, a healthy serving
of peach cobbler will have you changing careers and heading
west just to get yourself one more morsel of this cowboy treat.

PEACH COBBLER
Ingredients: Filling

1 cup butter

6 cups peeled and sliced fresh peaches

1 cup granulated sugar

1 cup brown sugar

1 teaspoon cinnamon

½ cup high-quality whiskey

Directions

Melt the butter in a Dutch oven. Add the peaches, granulated sugar,
brown sugar, and cinnamon. Bring mixture to a boil, then simmer for
15 minutes. Add the whiskey and cook for 15 to 20 minutes.

Ingredients: Crust

2 cups flour

1 teaspoon sugar

1 teaspoon salt

¾ cups shortening

¼ cup water

1 tablespoon cider vinegar

Directions

Combine the flour, sugar, and salt. Cut in the shortening until the mixture resembles coarse crumbs. Combine the water and vinegar and pour them into the flour mixture. Mix until ingredients hold together; the dough will be sticky. Cover and chill for 2 hours. Then, on a floured surface, roll out the dough to the size of the Dutch oven. Place the pastry sheet over the cooked fruit mixture and bake at 350 degrees for 45 minutes, or until the crust is golden brown.

If you are cooking outdoors, place the Dutch oven on moderate-size bed of coals and pile 2 to 3 times that amout of coals on the lid. Bake 40 to 45 minutes, or until the crust is golden brown.

We'd tell you to wash it down with a steaming hot cup of cowboy coffee, but you'll be awake until the first Tuesday of next month if you're not accustomed to it. Moreover, we know that your range boss wouldn't approve of that. But, when you get the chance, please take the time to enjoy it, because it just might be the one thing in a maddening day that sets your mind at ease and brings you the sweetest of dreams.

Although we'd love to leave you believing that the dishes we've talked about here were the be-all and end-all to the cowboy's dining existence, that wouldn't be true. There are dozens and dozens of dishes that Cookie used to create every morning, noon, and night to keep his cowboys satisfied. But as it so happens, one of the greatest delicacies in the cowboy's world was one that Cookie had nothing to do with.

MOUNTAIN OYSTERS

Remember the discussion we had about branding early on in your education on being a rancher? Then you also might recall a description of castration. In the cowboy world, nothing goes to waste, and that's precisely the case with castrated testicles. Cowboys call these delicacies "mountain oysters."

MOUNTAIN OYSTERS
Ingredients

1 pound calf testicles, or "mountain oysters"

2 eggs

Salt

Flour

Oil

Directions

Clean the oysters by placing them in boiling water for one minute. Remove them from the water and slice their membrane with a knife, separating the meat from the membrane. Then cut the oysters into ¼-inch slices, salt them, and dip them into beaten eggs. Dredge them in flour and fry them in oil until golden brown.

Cowboys cook 'em, eat 'em, and love 'em, and you'd be surprised how many city slickers enjoy them, too—that is, until they find out what they are. But if you can put that aside, we guarantee that if you like fried food, you'll love adding these to your repertoire.

Now, real-deal ranchers eat mountain oysters almost as fast as the testicles come off the bull calf. They cook them right over the coals of the branding fire, add a little salt, pop them in their mouths, and savor the flavor. But since most folks can't get them that fresh, and don't have a branding fire handy, they batter and fry them to a crisy morsel that will make you wonder why you didn't try them sooner. Once you've eaten one, in no time at all you'll be begging your butcher to get his hands on some for you to serve up at your next cookout. Don't worry. We'll let you have all the fun telling your guests what they've eaten once the whole batch has been devoured. Just be ready with your camera for their expressions—and send them to us!

★ COWBOY LAW

Just because cowboys live, work, and play among horses, cows, and other wild things, it doesn't mean they don't have manners. On the contrary, when it comes to dining at the chuck wagon or cookshack cowboys have always followed a strict code. Here are a few of the many rules of etiquette they've lived by:

1. Eat your food without waiting for the others. This makes for quicker service at the chuck wagon, and it allows the cowboy to get back to work sooner. And that's the mark of a good hand.
2. Never do anything to stir up dust around the chuck wagon, since no one wants a mouthful of dirt on their biscuits or in their beans.
3. Don't take the last of anything unless you are certain that everyone else has eaten.
4. Put your dishes in the "wreck," or dishpan, when done eating.
5. If you are refilling your coffee and someone calls out, "Man at the pot," you are obligated to refill everyone's coffee.
6. If the water barrel is empty when you get a drink, you are obligated to refill it.
7. Never, ever charge a stranger for a meal, and a stranger should never offer to pay. Both are insults in the cowboy's world.

By now, the cowboy's stomach is just about ready to burst, so it's time to do our version of cleaning up. Throughout our discussion of Cookie and his chuck wagon cooking, we've focused largely on history and food. However, these would mean nothing without one essential ingredient: hospitality.

As it was for Cookie a century and a half ago, food is nothing without good company. And good company is nothing without a host willing to go out of his way to make the dining experience pleasureable. Despite his outwardly rugged and oftentimes ornery demeanor, there was never a question in any cowboy's mind that Cookie cared about them and did his darnedest to make sure that everyone who entered his camp walked away for the better. Cowboys would not be who they are without Cookie, and Cookie would not be who he is without cowboys and food. And when all the pots and pans are washed, and the coals are nothing more than ash, we hope it's clear that in the cowboy's life, as it should be in anyone's life, every meal is a cause for celebration.

REAL-DEAL PROFILE

Whether they're wrangling corporate executives, inquisitive tourists, or cowboys-in-the-making while performing their duties as the proprietors of the M Lazy C Ranch in Lake George, Colorado, Randy and Brenda Myers understand that creating wonderful memories for their visitors is all about hospitality.

It doesn't matter if they're serving up tasty chuck wagon fare, gathering cows with a crew of "green" hands, or chatting the evening away with some New Yorkers, these two cowboys-at-heart go above and beyond the call of duty to make any and all who set foot upon their spread feel welcome.

They know that their work would not be complete if they did not do their damnedest to make sure that the people who spend time with them return to their homes and show the same hospitality to their guests as Randy and Brenda have shown them.

Brenda and Randy Myers

SIX

The Cowboy's Off-Hours

KICKING BACK WHEN THE WORK DAY'S THROUGH

There's no doubt the American cowboy loves working hard, whether it's mending a fence, pushing cattle, or riding the rodeo circuit. And most real-deal cowboys can keep hammering away at their chores at a feverish pace for lengthy periods of time without respite—many because they like it; some because they have to. But there's no question that from time to time every cowboy has to place his rope down, put on a clean shirt and jeans, scrape the mud off his boots, throw his finest hat atop his head, and depart from the rigors and solitude of ranch life.

But just where does the cowboy go to get away from it all?

Well, outside of home or ranch, there are two main places where cowboys congregate for social purposes: saloons and dance halls. These two types of establishments have deeply rooted histories that satisfy particular needs for the modern-day working cowboy, just as they did in the 1800s. Although it may seem like saloons and dance halls are one and the same, failing to differentiate between the two would be the equivalent of deeming all cattle to be Herefords when there are many varieties of cattle on the range.

COWBOY TRIVIA

History has it that the first saloon was established in 1822 as Brown's Hole near the Colorado, Utah, and Wyoming borders.

This topic is already making us thirsty, so let's get moving.

THE SALOON

The most logical place to start is the saloon, since it's what television and motion pictures have conditioned many of us to envision when we think of a cowboy heading to town for a little rest and relaxation. A saloon is what most city folk would call a bar or a tavern—nothing more, nothing less. Mind you, the first saloons were nothing too extravagant. On more occasions

than not, they were makeshift tents or lean-tos. It wasn't until many years later that they became more permanent structures that had the swinging doors and long mahogany bars that have made them so famously recognizable. Yet, no matter how rugged and rudimentary a saloon's appearance might have been, it was for the cowboy an almost perfect oasis of enjoyment, far away from the inherent stresses of life on the range.

SALOONS YOU'VE JUST GOT TO DRINK AT

Buffalo Chip Saloon and Steakhouse, Cave Creek, Arizona; Buckhorn Bar, Laramie, Wyoming; The Mint Bar, Sheridan, Wyoming

More specifically, the saloon served as a place where a cowboy could partake of three things: whiskey, women,

and gambling . . . but not necessarily in that order. The first and second were scarce as scarce could be on the range, so the cowboy had no choice but to battle the elements and journey into town to imbibe in such delights. As for the third, well, cowboys didn't have much money, so they took what little they had and ventured into town with the goal of winning it away from those who did. Although certain aspects of these three activities have since become illegal in most places, cowboys from far and wide still travel to saloons with the same ultimate intentions: to unwind in whatever way they see fit, so long as their endeavors fit within the confines of the law, of course. Don't make us tell you how the range boss would react if he found out that any of his hands spent their free time in the luxurious accommodations of the local county lock-up. We'll say this much: It won't be pretty.

ROCCO SAYS

Although movies and television often paint the picture of cow towns welcoming cowboys with open and loving arms, history tells a different story. More often than not, businessmen in cow towns were ruthless in their pursuit of separating the cowboy from his money, and would do almost anything to achieve that objective.

Now, we're not telling you that all cowboys are saints. We'd be lying to you if we did, and we don't take too kindly to not being truthful. But you have to understand that the pressure under which cowboys lived in the 1800s was almost insurmountable, literally a matter of life or death at every turn. Between cattle rustlers, mountain lions, rattlesnakes, drought, a cattle market that dropped faster than a boulder off the edge of the Grand Canyon, and a whole host of other concerns, the cowboy never seemed to catch a break. Accordingly, it was no wonder that when the cowboys received their monthly pay, they bolted for the nearest saloon, and, in the process, developed a reputation for raising some hell. But, contrary to popular opinion, there was nowhere near as much trouble at these establishments as people have been led to believe. Sure, there was an occasional gambling misunderstanding where a gun was used to settle the score, and some saloons had their front windows broken out during a fight. However, these were the exceptions. Cowboys so thoroughly enjoyed the pastime of heading to the saloon that they wouldn't have wanted to do anything that would prevent them from enjoying this escape when the opportunity arose.

 COWBOY TRIVIA

When you consider that virtually every cattle drive was alcohol- and woman-free, it's no wonder that when the drive was over, some sixty to ninety days after it began, cowboys literally raced into town to find some female companionship and elixir to help ease the troubles they'd experienced on the lonesome and treacherous range.

In situations where the cowboys were tempted to get a bit out of control to blow off steam, the lawmen and saloon owners were there to keep them in line. For example, in some cases, the lawmen prevented cowboys from carrying firearms into saloons, and some saloon keepers watered down the drinks as the night moved on, to prevent anyone from stepping over the prescribed boundaries of public drunkenness. But on most occasions, the cowboys looked out for one another.

Although saloons aren't the institutions they once were, they still exist all across the West, still providing a perfect place for the cowboy to whet his dusty whistle with a cold beer and a shot of whiskey if the occasion calls for it and to socialize with cowboys and non-cowboys alike.

COWBOY TRIVIA

Back in the early days of the cowboy, the cowpuncher's card game of choice was faro.

DANCE HALLS

Cowpokes also frequent what are called dance halls, direct offshoots of the ballrooms where people congregated to dance in the 1800s. Dance halls are much larger than saloons and regularly feature cowboy music that begs folks to get up and dance, which, as the name suggests, is the main

purpose of attending such establishments. There's one distinguishing feature that will tell you for certain that you're in a dance hall: a huge wooden dance floor. It's the be-all and end-all reason for going to one. In modern times, dance halls have become much more than simply places to dance. In many, you'll find everything from pool tables to high-end hatters, and many include restaurants that serve chuck wagon fare, while others feature live amateur bull riding events, making some of the more famous—or infamous, depending on your point of view—of these institutions a sort of amusement park for the cowboy.

THE WORLD'S BEST DANCE HALLS

Billy Bob's Texas, Fort Worth, Texas; The Grizzly Rose, Denver, Colorado

Yet, despite their differences, saloons and dance halls share one important ingredient: alcohol, in particular, beer and whiskey. And like the places where they they are enjoyed these two mainstays of the cowboy's world have historical significance for him.

COWBOY TRIVIA

The chuck wagon cook kept a bottle of whiskey on the wagon under lock and key at all times, for its use was reserved strictly for medicinal purposes.

DRINKING

Whiskey is a spirit that can be distilled virtually anywhere using a wide array of base ingredients, including barley, wheat, and corn. The distillation process is simple to replicate, which avoids the necessity of demanding master distillers to produce it. This doesn't mean that all whiskey is created the same. Back in the day, there were those distillers who produced whiskey as smooth and satisfying as Cookie's peach cobbler, but there were also those whose whiskey was better used as paint remover. In many cases, the quality of the whiskey was in direct proportion to the price paid for it. Yet there were those underhand saloonkeepers who did their best to pass off bad whiskey at a premium price. Needless to say, cowboys didn't take too kindly to this. When they had the money in their pockets to have a drink, which in itself was rare, they wanted quality, and saloonkeeper had to beware if they tried to compromise on that! This is one area where the cowboy's view has not changed one iota since he came into existence.

COWBOY TRIVIA

Cowboys used to refer to whiskey as "throat oil," "neck warmer," and "gut warmer," along with a host of other colorful names.

HOW TO DRINK LIKE A COWBOY

Pour one ounce of high-quality whiskey into a shot glass, then remove an ice-cold beer from the cooler. Pop the cap off of the beer, then down the whiskey and enjoy the beer.

Besides whiskey, you'll often find cowboys drinking ice-cold beer. However, beer is a modern luxury when compared with whiskey, as it was not widely available across cowboy country until the railroads arrived, being difficult to store and even more troublesome to transport. Furthermore, it's been argued that brewing a tolerable beer was a bit trickier than brewing a tolerable whiskey. We're not sure if whiskey distillers would agree, but we'd venture to guess that the cowboy's tolerance for whiskey over beer might have to do with the fact that the cowboy was simply more accustomed to whiskey—good, bad, and horrendous.

Nevertheless, there's no question that you'll find real-deal cowboys indulging in both beer and whiskey when the occasion calls for it, as infrequent as that may be, considering all the higher priorities that dominate their world. It's one of those areas where there's no need to go searching for something new to drink. When you've got a good thing going, why spoil it?

COWBOY MUSIC

Now that you've got a drink in hand, and you've settled into your off-the-ranch surroundings, it's time we introduce you to the next installment in the cowboy's repertoire of free-time activities: cowboy music.

COWBOY MUSICIANS YOU'VE GOT TO HEAR

Sons of the San Joaquin; Tex Ritter; R. W. Hampton

It's critical to understand that when we say cowboy music, we don't mean what's popularly known as country music, more specifically, the kind of music often associated with Nashville. The type of music that finds its Mecca in Nashville evolved from the cowboy music of the mid- to late-1800s, so it's more appropriately defined as a distant cousin to cowboy music, rather than the same thing. This is not to say that country music does not play a role in the cowboy's life, as more often than not you'll find a cowpuncher's truck radio tuned in to the local station that plays all the top country hits of the day. Hell, Johnny Cash, Waylon Jennings, Willie Nelson, and Brad Paisley happen to be some of our favorite country musicians, but we'd bet that even they'll tell you they don't play "cowboy music" as we're defining it here. In order to provide you with the most authentic look into cowboy life we're going to stick with the roots of his music, which, as you might have guessed, happens to be alive and well today—all because of the cowboys of yesteryear.

★ COWBOY LAW

It's an unwritten rule among cowboys that a song or poem is not to be interrupted unless the song or poem itself is the subject matter of the particular discussion.

THE GUITAR

We're going to work into this subject by first giving you the inside scoop on the tools of the cowboy musician's trade. Most folks would probably argue that the guitar is the most important piece of equipment in the cowboy musician's instrument cabinet. In certain scenarios, that's correct, but in others, it's dead wrong.

There's no doubt that the guitar plays a vital role in the performance of cowboy music. We've all seen photos of a cowboy with guitar in hand sitting next to a campfire picking and singing a song to his fellow hands. But this was a common occurrence only when cowboys were at home on the ranch or sleeping near the chuck wagon during a cattle drive, since the guitar is too clunky an instrument to haul onto the range.

Wherever he used it, whenever the cowboy had a guitar in his hand, it was a real treat. He could play a song that would make the rest of the cattlemen cry, or he could break into a fast-paced ditty that would get the other cowboys up and dancing. The guitar was a tool whose uses were limited only by the hands of the cowboy playing it.

THE COWBOY'S CHOICE FOR MUSICAL INSTRUMENTS
C. F. Martin Guitars and Hohner Harmonicas

THE HARMONICA
In many cases the cowboy didn't have the luxury of having a guitar to entertain the other cowboys. When that was the case, he would break out an equally essential piece of equipment: the harmonica.

The harmonica, or mouth harp, held wide appeal because it could easily be transported and could produce a sound so beautiful that it was hard to imagine an instrument that could compare out on the range. However, the harmonica was not played only for the benefit of other cowboys. Nope. The cowboy spread the wealth.

When he was the nighthawk, that is, the cowboy who kept

an eye on the cattle throughout the night, the cowboy would tuck his prized harmonica in his shirt pocket and take it with him. As he rode his horse among the cattle, he'd softly play the harmonica to help calm them. There's not a cowman from Mexico to Canada who won't tell you that the harmonica's lullaby has prevented many a stampede and helped many a cowboy on duty pass many a lonesome and cold night.

Yet, even if a cowboy had a guitar or harmonica, it didn't necessarily mean that cowboy music would result. To make that happen, the cowboy needed a song.

HOME ON THE RANGE

Version by John A. Lomax (1910; guitar chords in parentheses)

Verse

    (G)   (C)

Oh, give me a home, where the buffalo roam,

        (G)   (A7)   (D7)

Where the deer and the antelope play,

    (G)   (C)

Where seldom is heard a discouraging word,

    (G)   (D7)   (G)

And the skies are not cloudy all day.

Chorus

(G)   (D7)   (G)

Home, home on the range,

             (A7)   (D7)

Where the deer and the antelope play,

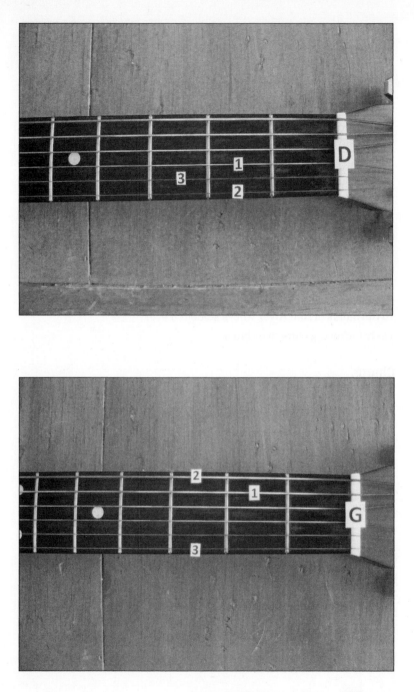

```
        (G)                    (C)
Where seldom is heard a discouraging word,

        (G)           (D7)      (G)
And the skies are not cloudy all day.
```

Where the air is so pure, the zephyrs so free,
The breezes so balmy and light,
That I would not exchange my home on the range
For all the cities so bright.

Chorus

The red man was pressed from this part of the West,
He's likely no more to return
To the banks of Red River where seldom if ever
Their flickering campfires burn.

Chorus

How often at night when the heavens are bright
With the light from the glittering stars
Have I stood here amazed and asked as I gazed
If their glory exceeds that of ours.

Chorus

Oh, I love these wild prairies where I roam
The curlew I love to hear scream,
And I love the white rocks and the antelope flocks
That graze on the mountain-tops green.

Chorus

Oh, give me a land where the bright diamond sand
Flows leisurely down the stream,
Where the graceful white swan goes gliding along
Like a maid in a heavenly dream.

Chorus

You might be thinking that a few catchy lines and a chorus that you can't get out of your head make for a good song. But in order for a song to be classified as an honest-to-goodness cowboy song, the lyrics have to tell a story. And we're not talking some kitschy story about something that has no meaning. We're talking about words that have significance. In fact, and almost by definition, a cowboy song has to convey a story from a real-deal cowboy's perspective. For those of us who don't live and die on the range, that presents a problem. Actually, it presents a problem even for many real-deal cowboys today, because many of the lyrics in old-time cowboy songs contain colloquialisms that are almost impossible to comprehend without performing in-depth research. And even that may not provide you with the information you need for comprehension. But when you can decipher the meaning of the lyrics, you are in for a memory you will never forget—a gift from cowboys who roamed the range over a hundred years ago.

MUST-HEAR DANCE HALL MUSICIANS FOR YOUR PLAYLIST
Pat James; Robert Earl Keen; Jerry Jeff Walker

DANCING

Although the cowboy musician loves nothing more than to spend an entire evening playing the most heartfelt of melodies, none worth the saddle he rides upon would consider placing his harmonica or guitar back in its case until he dished up an ample number of tunes that caused his audience to tap their heels, jump up off their seats, and start dancing. For those of you who are chomping at the bit to hit the dance floor, God bless you. By the time you get through this section, you'll be raring to go. And for those of you who claim you can't dance or are as timid as a baby cow before the branding iron, it's time to change that attitude and partake in this most fundamental of cowboy off-hour endeavors. We don't have time for weak-minded people on the range. So get out there and dance. And don't worry. We'll be right there next to you showing you how it's done—or, as luck would have it, how it's not done.

 COWBOY TRIVIA
If you think you're too tough to dance, guess again. Seven-time World Champion All-Around Cowboy and "King of the Cowboys" Ty Murray danced his way to stardom on the floor of ABC's hit television show *Dancing with the Stars*.

To be clear, when we say dance, we mean what's called country and western dance, which encompasses a broad array of dance styles, patterns, and techniques. This type of dancing didn't just pop up out of nowhere. Like most everything else in the world of cowboys, it is rooted deeply in history.

When immigrants settle in the United States, they bring with them their languages, customs, and cultures. One of the gems they bring from the old country is dance, which in the 1700s and 1800s included solo dances such as the jig, couple dances such as the minuet and the schottische, group dances such as the grand march, single-line dances, and square dances. And when these folks moved west in search of freedom and new beginnings, they brought their dances with them. The music and styles largely formalized in Europe then merged with conjunto music from northern Mexico, ultimately forming the basis of modern-day country and western dance.

COWBOY TRIVIA

When no women were around, cowboys held "stag" dances, in which a scarf was tied around one of the dancer's arms to designate that he had been "heifer-branded," or selected to play the role of the woman in the partnered dance.

Dance is, and always has been, a way for people to express themselves, socialize, exercise, and have some plain old-fashioned fun. During their limited off-hours, old-time cowboys organized balls, cotillions, "Germans," hops, and "fandangos." Sometimes announcements were made in the local newspaper, but more often than not, notice of such events was spread by word of mouth. At other times, cowboys would just start dancing, and pretty soon everyone around them would join in. Dancing was one of the few means for the cowboy to obtain some relief from the multitude of struggles he faced daily at every turn.

ROCCO SAYS

Real cowboys don't line-dance.

Although we could spend a great deal of time talking about line dancing and other forms of dance, we're going to concentrate on the three most common forms of modern-day partner dancing: the two-step, triple-step, and waltz. Frankly, those line dances are a little too tricky for us to explain, and because they are ever evolving, by the time you're done reading this book, a whole new wave of line dances will most likely have overtaken country and western dance floors across America.

DANCIN' TRIVIA

Dance is one realm where formality still reigns supreme. On dance floors all across the West, men are referred to at all times as gentlemen, and the women are referred to at all times as ladies. In the world of real-deal cowboys, that's one tradition that has never been broken.

DANCIN' TRIVIA

In many dance halls across the West, you'll find sawdust or cornmeal scatterefd across the dance floor. This is spread around to allow the dancers to slide their boots across the floor with greater ease.

DIRECTION AND THE DANCE FLOOR

The country and western dance floor operates like a horse track, where, just like race horses, dancers move in a counterclockwise direction, circling the perimeter, as the middle of the dance floor is reserved for line dancing and other forms of partner dancing. In addition, dancers do not circle the dance floor in a single-file line. Rather, they form different lanes, just like racehorses, so they don't run into each other.

COWBOY LAW

In order to guarantee the success of a dance, the gentleman and lady should adhere to the following principles: One, the footwork must be correct. Two, the gentleman is the leader; the lady is the follower. Three, the dancers must move in rhythm to the music. And, four, the gentleman must plan where he desires to lead his lady.

Most often you'll find that a gentleman will approach a lady, extend his hand, and request a dance. She has two choices: politely decline, or accept. If she accepts, she places her hand in his, and he leads her to the dance floor.

The couple then assumes what's called the "dance frame," or the means through which the dancers connect to each other with their hands and arms. It is essential that the dancers maintain a firm dance frame throughout the dance, because it's the only way a gentleman can correctly lead, and a lady correctly follow, during a given dance sequence. After connecting with the lady, the gentleman tells her which dance they will performing: the two-step, triple-step, or waltz.

ROCCO SAYS

When dancing with a lady, reserve the "vise" grip for steer wrestling.

We'd love to illustrate the footwork here, but the plain old truth is that we'd just confuse you. So do us a favor and find a qualified instructor who'll teach you right.

DANCIN' KNOW-HOW

Determining which dance to perform is often simply a matter of how the gentleman "hears" the music. Sometimes a song in four-four time may sound perfect for a two-step, while at others, there is no question that the triple-step is more suitable.

THE TWO STEP

The two-step is the most common form of partner dancing and is performed in four-four time—that is, to music containing four beats per measure. In this dance, the dancers literally walk across the dance floor in a quick-quick-slow-slow pattern. What this means is that the couple takes two quick steps followed by two slower steps, with each step taking place in time to the music. No matter what the pace of the music, all of the steps should be the same size. This is what's called the "basic" step, or the footwork that forms the basis of all of the more complicated dance moves—the spins, turns, poses, and more. We'd love to show you how to take this basic step to the expert level, but there's no substitute for hands-on instruction from a qualified dance professional.

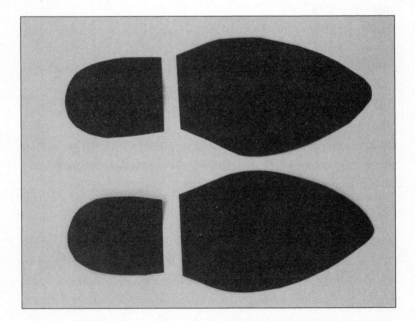

When dancing to faster-paced music, take smaller steps. This will provide for better control and allow you to execute more complicated moves with greater ease.

THE TRIPLE STEP

As it turns out, the next song the band plays brings with it a beat perfect for the triple-step, which is the second most common step in country and western dance. Like the two-step, the triple-step is danced in four-four time. There's no replacement for this style of dance when the music and the beat get your blood pumping. This dance is similar to the polka, except rather than dancing to German Oktoberfest-style music, dancers move in rhythm to cowboy music. Here, the basic steps for the gentleman make a left-and-left, right-and-right pattern. There are two keys to this dance: one, the feet should slide across the dance floor (as opposed to simply stepping, as with the two-step), and, two, the hips should be allowed to turn freely from side to side in time with the rhythm of the feet. The natural turning of the hips creates a bounce, giving this dance its signature look on the dance floor. Again, there are many variations on this basic dance step. In fact, the exact same moves that can be performed in the two-step can be performed in the triple-step, so once you learn the two-step, the triple-step becomes second nature.

THE WALTZ

Now that you've learned the fundamentals of the two dances that take place in four-four time, we're ready to move on to the most common dance that takes place in three-four time—that is, to music containing three beats per measure. We're talking about the waltz—arguably the most graceful of all the country and western dances.

REAL-DEAL PROFILE

The man who coined the expression "You can't teach an old dog new tricks" apparently never met country and western dance instructor Dennis Guillian.

Dennis wrangles cowboys and cowboy wanna-bes into his classes at the Grizzly Rose in Denver, Colorado, where he shows them the ropes for everything from the Texas two-step to the waltz to the West Coast swing. It doesn't matter if his students are young or old, novice or expert, by the time Dennis is finished with them, they have the skills to take their newfound knowledge onto any sawdust-strewn dance floor in America.

Dennis instills in his students not only a sense of accomplishment and happiness, but also an appreciation for the simple pleasures that have been part and parcel of nearly every cowboy's life since the 1860s.

The waltz pattern follows what's called a "hard one, soft two, three," or a "heel, ball, ball" format. As with the two-step and triple-step, it is from this basic waltz step that more complicated moves and patterns can be created. This basic step is best described by as having a "rise and fall" quality—that is, the dancers appear to be rising and falling on the dance floor like the waves of the ocean. We don't think there's any dance prettier to watch than this one.

We'll tell you what. We're plum worn out from explaining all this to you, so we're going to head home and build ourselves a nice campfire. We'd love for you to join us, because if you do, you're in for a real treat. In fact, if you come with us, we wager our best cutting horses that you'll feel like you've traveled back in time to the golden age of the cattle drive. But to do so, we need some help from the only man who can take us there—the cowboy poet.

Dennis Guillian

COWBOY POETRY

Cowboy poetry is a not exactly the type of poetry that many of us are accustomed to hearing, where emphasis is placed on structure and rhyme. The most important characteristic of a cowboy poem is that it tell a story. It doesn't always follow a logical structure, and its meter can be as erratic as a bull storming out of a bucking shoot, but without exception, it tells a story. Remembering this rule will serve you many times over when you make time to delve into a volume of this type of literature.

MUST-HEAR COWBOY POETS

Don Edwards; Red Steagall; Waddie Mitchell

 COWBOY TRIVIA
Every winter, cowboy poets gather in Elko, Nevada, for the National Cowboy Poetry Gathering, which showcases everyone from up-and-coming performers to modern-day legends, both providing the audience with an experience that is not soon forgotten.

But old-time poetry didn't appear in books. You see, back in the day, many cowboys—and people in general—didn't have the education we have today. This meant that few people could read or write, which presented a problem; poetry books were of little or no value if people couldn't read them. As a result, folks needed someone with creativity, a good memory, and exceptional performance skills to pass on to future generation these true, and sometimes semi-true and untrue, stories.

DREAM

We're not poets of the West.

Most of us are just working to do our best.

Did you notice that you're more a cow than a cowboy, like many are today?

Herded off to work and back, longing for simpler ways.

The range you ride is concrete hard; your work is just routine.

But in that little cubicle, your mind is free to dream,

Of a cold sunrise and the short grass wet with dew,

The air filled with chill as you grab a cup of brew.

Bacon and eggs sizzling on the campfire, the biscuits cooked up golden brown.

Then the camp cook yells, "Come and get it!" All the cowboys gather around.

You can see the cattle moving, and hear the top hand swear,

"Let's get moving!" And you climb on that saddled mare.

"We're burning daylight here!"

And you take off a chasing some old Longhorn steer.

You can feel that horse beneath ya as your loop swings through the air

The ponies' hot breath blowing across your face and through your hair

When suddenly you're caught up short by a ringing telephone.

That brings you back to the place were your life is not your own.

But now when you want to escape, it's over mountains, past cactus and through streams,

To where there are some real cowboys waiting to ride with you in your dreams.

Look at those cowboys; on there faces you'll see a smile,

Listen closely to the words they speak, thank you Lord for letting those fine folks be a cowboy for awhile.

Lines to Use to Try Your Hand at Cowboy Poetry

_____

_____

_____

_____

_____

_____

_____

_____

_____

_____

_____

_____

_____

_____

_____

_____

_____

_____

_____

_____

_____

_____

_____

_____

_____

Enter the cowboy poet, the revered storyteller of every cow camp in America. Whether before an audience in town, sitting around a campfire, or standing around during a brief water break while on the range, the cowboy poet might break into verse, orally conveying poems that were taught to him, along with those he composed himself based on his own experiences. His audience, be they non-cowboys or his closest of cowpuncher friends, would listen to his words with the tenacity of children hoping to hear Santa's sleighbells on Christmas Eve. The perfectly woven and crafted tales would remind them of the way it once was and keep them current on the events of the day. At times the poems made them think; at others they made them laugh; and at others, they made them cry. It was the cowboy poet's ability to touch the emotions of the listener that made him such a treasure far and wide.

Cowboy poets of today carry on this tradition. Like rodeo cowboys, many cowboy poets have given up full-time ranching duties to pursue the path they love and, in the process, have brought joy to every ear open to the experience. As a matter of fact, we're half grinning and half holding back our tears as we recall some of our favorite lines and performances.

We swore we wouldn't cry while writing this book, so we'd better change the topic before we need to borrow your wild rag to clear up our eyes.

And as the ranch would have it, there's no better time to call it a night than right now, because daybreak's only a few hours away, and with it comes a whole new list of chores that need attending to. But before we head off to our bedrolls to catch a few hours of sleep prior to sunrise, we want to leave you with a thought that we hope will serve you throughout your entire lives: The cowboy *survives* because he works hard at what he's been called to do, but the cowboy *thrives*

Dick Huntzinger

because he makes the time to break from his daily routine to experience all the pleasures life has to offer. It is through this devotion to making the most of his off-hours that the cowboy comes to enjoy himself, his family, his friends, and those who soon will be his friends. That is the difference between having a life and living one.

REAL-DEAL PROFILE

Dick Huntzinger eats, breathes, and sleeps the cowboy lifestyle each and every day of his life. If he's not working cattle, he's developing ways to rehabilitate horses, and if he's not doing either of those, it's almost certain you'll hear him reciting cowboy poetry—those colorful tales of Western lore passed on from generation to generation.

Whether his story's about lassoing a bear, chasing your dreams, or pushing cattle through a blizzard, Dick's rhythmical and enchanting voice causes any listener to close his eyes and feel as if he were transported back to the heyday of the American cowboy.

However, the magic comes not so much from the words themselves, but from the soul with which they are spoken—and Dick's cowboy soul is bigger than the landmass of the Louisiana Purchase.

Not only does Dick's simple way of conveying profound thoughts bring joy to those fortunate enough to hear him, they bring life to a treasured part of our country's history. And it is by continuing this tradition that cowboys the world over will be remembered and revered for years to come.

SEVEN
Rodeo

THE ART OF WILD DREAMS, WILDER MEN, AND THE WILDEST OF RIDES

While most kids in America dream of growing up to play in the NFL or the NBA, cowboy kids dream of one day riding the perfect eight-second, one-hundred-point championship bull in the last round of the National Finals Rodeo and taking home the buckle for winning the All-Around Cowboy title. And though rodeo life may seem like a simple transition from growing up on a ranch, winning, and winning consistently, is anything but simple.

RODEO TRIVIA
There's a saying in rodeo: Only the dead stay down.

To explain it all, we'll walk you through the two types of rodeo in our discussion. The first is what we'll call conventional rodeo, which is the type of rodeo that most of us know, with its bull and bronc riding, steer wrestling, barrel racing, and more. This is the rodeo where you could say the athletes of the cowboy world compete. Then there's what's called ranch rodeo, which encompasses events that are more akin to the work you'd see on a ranch, such as cow cutting, branding, team penning, and other events. This is where the working ranch cowboy finds his battle. We're going to provide you with a behind-the-grandstands look at both types of rodeo, since each plays an integral role in the cowboy's life. But to better appreciate both types of rodeo, it helps to understand how rodeo began.

RODEO MUST-READ

Rodeo in America: Wranglers, Roughstock, and Paydirt, by Wayne S. Wooden and Gavin Ehringer

In the mid-1800s, during the advent of the cattle industry, the cowboy spent the majority of the year working the cattle on the ranches and rangelands of the West. There, he relied upon his roping and riding skills during roundups, moving herds, and branding to get the job at hand done as efficiently and effectively as possible. It quickly became apparent that some cowboys were more proficient than others at roping, riding, and handling horses and livestock. Cowboys within a cow camp and from different cow camps had their own opinions about who truly was the best man on the ranch. But talk didn't mean a whole lot on the range. The only way for a man to prove himself was through a competition.

In the early years, cowboys informally gathered and placed bets on the cowboy who could rope and ride the best. Competition was fierce, and winning was less about money and more about pride.

As the cattle industry grew, so did the number of cowboys who participated in such gatherings. Eventually cowboys realized that a bit more organization was required to manage these events.

Enter the rodeo.

Rodeo, which is derived from the Spanish word *rodear*, meaning round up, was the quintessential means for cowboys to display their skills to an audience and prove once and for all who was top in any given event. Rules were introduced, and participation slowly became a full-time occupation for some. The events grew from small-town rodeos to mega-performances in places such as Cheyenne, Prescott, Pendleton, and Houston, which attracted hundreds of rodeo cowboys and thousands of dollars in prize money. As a result, rodeo became a full-fledge athletic endeavor.

And though, as with every other sport, rodeo has transformed over time, there is no question that its importance to the cowboy's competitive and social life has remained the same over the last 150 years—same broken bones, same broken heads, same broken hearts.

ROCCO SAYS

Rodeo is one of few sports that started out as a job and turned into a sport, whereas mainstream sports, such as football and baseball, started out as sports and turned into jobs.

CONVENTIONAL RODEO

In rodeo, as in virtually every experience in life, you have to understand a few things to start your experience off on the right horseshoe. Here's the lowdown on conventional rodeo.

In the world of conventional rodeo, two main governing bodies oversee the sport: the Professional Rodeo Cowboys Association, or the PRCA, and Professional Bull Riders, Inc., or the PBR. The PRCA has roots that reach back decades to the advent of organized rodeo competitions, whereas the PBR is a relatively new endeavor, having begun in the late

1900s. The main difference between the two organizations is that the PRCA serves as the governing body for all professional rodeo events, while the PBR specializes in bull riding.

In order to compete in a PRCA-sanctioned event, a rodeo cowboy must obtain what's called a PRCA "card." To do this, he must first earn a certain amount of prize money on a PRCA "permit," the equivalent of a driver's permit. But even after receiving his card, a rodeo cowboy doesn't just jump on a horse or bull and enter an event straightaway. He first must adhere to strictly enforced rules, such as paying an entry fee and wearing a longsleeve shirt, cowboy hat, and boots while performing. Yet these rules are rather insignificant when compared to the rule-of-all-rules, which *all* rodeo cowboys must abide by: the rodeo cowboy must act like a gentleman at all times in and outside the arena. No exceptions.

ROCCO SAYS

Unlike many sports we watch on television every day, there is no room for prima donnas in the rodeo arena. Not only would the fans show their disapproval, but the governing rules and rigors of the sport would make it virtually impossible for a prima donna cowboy to compete.

RODEO TRIVIA

The PRCA sanctions more than six hundred rodeos per year, while the PRB sanctions an annual three hundred plus bull riding events.

COWBOY TRIVIA

Rodeo cowboys are unique in that they cheer one another on, hoping everyone achieves his best performance every time he competes—even if cheering on another cowboy means that you might lose to him.

First of all, rodeo is not a competition; nor is it a game. It's not a round, and it's not a set. Real-deal rodeo cowboys call their pursuit a perf, which is short for performance. Historically, rodeo cowboys showed up at an arena to put on a performance for their fans and, in particular, their families, and the same largely remains true today. So now when you talk rodeo with someone, particularly someone well versed in the field, use that expression from the get-go and you'll be one trot closer to winning over the attention and heart of the cowboy who's listening.

 RODEO TRIVIA
Roughstock riders use long lengths of leather called spur straps or spur leathers to secure their spurs to their boots, preventing the spurs from flying off during the violence of an event. And many bareback and bull riders use the same types of straps, called latigos, to fasten their gloves to their wrists to prevent the gloves from slipping off during the event and causing them to lose their grip.

The sport of conventional rodeo is divided into two categories: roughstock events and timed events. Roughstock events include bareback, saddle bronc, and bull riding. Timed events include tie-down roping, team roping, steer wrestling, and barrel racing. All roughstock events follow the same guidelines: a rider must ride his "stock," or the bucking horse or bull, for eight seconds without being bucked off or disqualified, after which the rider receives a score from 1 to 100, based on the quality of the ride and the stock, with 100 being the best score possible. A timed event is judged based on the number of seconds it takes the cowboy to complete the event, with the lowest time winning, as long as the rider has not been disqualified from the event. Disqualifications occur for a number of reasons, which we'll explain in more detail as we walk you through the events.

ROCCO SAYS

Most folks outside the world of rodeo do not understand how many hours roughstock riders devote daily to working out simply in order to survive the exceptional demands of their events.

BEST-OF-THE-BEST RODEO SCHOOLS

Gary Leffew Bull Riding School; Joe Beaver Roping Schools

In the larger picture, rodeo cowboys participate in what are called "go-rounds," which are like the preliminary and finals competitions in other sports. The preliminary competition is called the long go-round, or long go, and is the stage at which the cowboy makes his initial perf in his chosen event or events. Commonly, riders receiving the best scores or times in the "long go" advance to the "short go-round," or the "short go," the equivalent of the finals. At the completion of the "short go," the cowboy with the best combined score or time wins the event.

RODEO TRIVIA

Rodeo cowboys also compete in what is known as the "slack" performance. The slack is usually held in the morning, well before the evening's main perf, and is used to narrow down the field when too many cowboys have entered a particular event.

Then the "All-Around Cowboy" is chosen. This title is earned by achieving the best performance in all of the events combined. For example, if one cowboy competes in saddle bronc and bull riding, and another cowboy competes in tie-down roping and steer wrestling, the dollar amount earnings for all of a cowboy's winnings in his chosen events are combined together, and the cowboy with the highest combined earnings wins the All-Around title, which is the equivalent of the Most Valuable Player award in mainstream sports. It is an extremely coveted title, for it signifies the rodeo cowboy's overall versatility and ability.

RODEO FILMS YOU'VE JUST GOT TO SEE

Rank (2006); *Adrenaline Cowboys* (2004); *8 Seconds* (1994)

COWBOY TRIVIA

In the roughstock events, the animals ridden are chosen by a "draw," or random lottery, in which a rider is matched up with a given horse or bull.

Now, you've got the overall concept in your head and you're sitting back, ready for the perf to begin. An introduction by the rodeo announcer, a hats-off for the singing of the National Anthem, and a yeehaw! later, the wild rides are set to begin.

BAREBACK RIDING

Generally, the first event is bareback riding. Here, the cowboy straps his hand into his rigging, a suitcase-like handle strapped to the horse's midsection. Once the rider has his hand in the handle just how he wants it, he leans back and signals for the gate to be opened. Once the gate swings wide, the cowboy must "mark out" the horse, or keep his heels above the horse's shoulders before the horse's front legs hit the ground in order to receive a "qualified ride," that is, a ride for which the rider can receive a score. The cowboy rides the horse for the required eight seconds and receives a score of 1 to 100 points.

RODEO TRIVIA

Bareback riding has been likened to strapping yourself to a rocket.

ROCCO SAYS

Hands down, bareback riding is the most physically demanding event in all of rodeo. It's like repeatedly getting into a violent car accident for eight seconds.

TIE-DOWN ROPING

After bareback, we head to the other end of the arena for tie-down roping. Tie-down roping is the ultimate battle between horse and rider and a fast-as-lighting calf. In this event, a calf is led into a chute, while a cowboy on horseback backs his horse into the "box," a three-side enclosure directly adjacent to the chute. The cowboy sticks his "pigin'" rope in his mouth, which we'll discuss in short order, and then pulls out his lariat and adjusts the loop to the desired size. When he is ready to begin, he nods to the person controlling the chute to release the calf, and the time clock begins. The calf gets a predetermined head start before the cowboy can exit the box. To control this, a "barrier," in the form of a length of rope, is strung across the opening of the box. This breaks away upon contact with the horse. The cowboy then explodes out of the box in pursuit of the calf. He swings the rope above his head and throws the loop around the calf's neck. Then he leaps from his horse—one that is moving at upwards of forty miles per hour—and sprints toward the calf. He wraps his arms around the calf's body and flanks the calf in much the same way hands do during the branding process. Then he removes the several-feet-long pigin' rope he's had clenched in his teeth all this time, and uses it to tie three of the calf's legs together. Once they're tied, the cowboy raises his hands, and the clock is stopped. The calf must remain secured for six seconds in order to receive a time. The roper with the lowest time wins.

If the cowboy "breaks the barrier," that is, if his horse crosses the length of rope before the calf gets its guaranteed head start, the rodeo cowboy is disqualified from the race and receives a "no score."

 RODEO TRIVIA
In tie-down roping, the rope the cowboy swings overhead is tied "hard and fast" to the horse, which means it is firmly secured to so that horse and calf are "permanently" connected to one another once the calf is roped.

SADDLE BRONC

Next comes the saddle bronc event. Here, riders use a modified version of the saddle that cowboys use on the range. However, instead of holding on to a pair of leather reins attached to a bridle, the rider grasps just one cotton rope that is secured to the horse's halter. Once the rider is on the saddle, with boots in the stirrups and the rein in his hand, he nods, and the gate swings open. The horse bucks and the rider feels out the horse, getting in sync with its movements. As he rides, the cowboy moves his legs back and forth in the stirrups for the duration of the ride in order to keep his balance and score points. At the end of eight seconds, the cowboy receives

a score based on much the same criteria as the saddle bronc. The rodeo cowboy with the highest score wins the go-round.

COWBOY TRIVIA

Steers grow horns much faster than their female counterparts.

RODEO TRIVIA

Saddle bronc has been called the "ballet" of rodeo, because of the grace and finesse required for a successful—and high-scoring—ride.

TEAM ROPING

After the poetry of the saddle bronc ride comes the event in rodeo that requires more teamwork than any other, and is aptly named team roping. In this event, two cowboys on horseback compete against one steer. The object is for one

of the cowboys to rope the steer around its head or horns (this cowboy is called a header) and the other to rope its legs (this cowboy is called the heeler). In theory, it sounds simple, but carrying this out is one of the most difficult tasks in rodeo, because of the many factors that come into play. We'll walk you through it just to show you how demanding the event truly is.

The header and heeler both back their horses into boxes

on opposite sides of the steer, which is positioned in a chute in the same way a calf is at the start of tie-down roping. The cowboys ready their ropes, and then the header nods to have the steer released. As with tie-down roping, the cowboys must allow the animal to get its predetermined head start before the chase begins. Then the cowboys take off after the steer. While the heeler lags behind, the header blasts ahead, riding up to the left flank of the animal and throwing his rope, preferably catching the animal around the horns. This provides greater control, although several other "catches" are legal, such as around the neck or around one horn and the head. The header then "dallys" the rope, or loops it one and a half times around the saddle horn to secure the steer to the horse via the rope. He then gracefully, but speedily, leads the steer to the left so that the heeler has a nice clean shot at roping the steer's hind legs. The heeler throws his rope, catches the hind legs, dallys the rope around the saddle horn, and both cowboys stop their horses. The time clock stops when the cowboys' horses face each other, after which the cowboys release their ropes, and the steer is set free to run another day, most likely a few weeks down the road.

COWBOY TRIVIA

The term *dally* comes from the Spanish phrase *dar la vuelta*, which translates "to take a turn."

STEER WRESTLING

If our description of team roping hasn't convinced you of the amount of coordination required to perform in rodeo, look no further than steer wrestling.

RODEO TRIVIA

Steer wrestling was originally called bulldogging. It earned its name because of a black cowboy named Bill Pickett, who, during the 101 Ranch Wild West Show of the early 1900s, brought down a steer by jumping onto it and biting its lip, just like a bulldog does.

Like team roping, steer wrestling makes use of two cowboys, two horses, and one steer that regularly weighs four hundred pounds or more. While both cowboys back their horses into the box, the steer is guided into the chute in between them. Generally, the cowboy on the left of the steer is the steer wrestler, while the cowboy on the right is known as the hazer.

Once the cowboys are backed into the box, the steer wrestler gives the nod to release the steer, and then allows the steer to get its running start. Then both cowboys bolt out after it. The hazer rides alongside the steer to make sure that it runs in a straight line to ensure that it remains in perfect position for the steer wrestler to perform his event.

 RODEO TRIVIA

It's been said that if you want to experience what it feels like to steer wrestle, climb in the back of a pickup truck, order the driver to slam down on the accelerator, and, when the speedometer reads forty miles per hour, jump out of the bed and tackle a telephone pole.

Now, while the hazer's doing his job, the steer wrestler rides up alongside the steer, removes his left foot from its stirrup, leans heavily toward the running steer, slides off his saddle, and in one fluid motion throws his body onto the steer, grabbing the steer's head and horns—all at a full gallop. The steer wrestler then digs his heels into the ground to stop the steer, while maneuvering the steer's head so that it and the cowboy fall to the ground, with both lying on their sides. Once the animal hits the ground and its legs are all pointed in the same direction, the clock stops. The cowboy stands up, dusts off his jeans, and the steer rises to his feet and meanders away. The lowest time wins.

BARREL RACING

Although there's no jumping off of animals in the next rodeo event, it is the event where speed is the order of the day. We're talking about barrel racing, which happens to be the only event in PRCA-sanctioned rodeos where women, and only women, compete.

Barrel racing is all about the connection between the rider and the horse. It doesn't matter if you are the world's greatest horseman if your horse doesn't want to listen to anything you're saying. The same holds true for the horse. If you've got a horse that instinctively knows how to win at barrel racing, but a rider who just doesn't get it, then the pair are in for a whole bunch of mediocre performances. But when horse and rider are in tune with each other and with the arena, watch out, because this is one exciting event.

In this event, three barrels are placed in the arena at the points of an imaginary triangle. The race begins and ends just in front of the imaginary base of the triangle, where an electronic-eye-style time clock, or the "eye," is placed.

RODEO TRIVIA

Barrel racing is governed by the Women's Professional Rodeo Association, which is the equivalent of the PRCA, under whose oversight all other events operate.

When the cowboy is ready, she spurs her horse and off they sprint, or run "wide open," toward the starting line. The rider heads for the barrel in the left base point of the triangle (although some riders begin with the right base point, as it's a matter of personal preference), and circles it as tightly as possible in a counterclockwise direction, and then bolts for the right base point of the triangle and rounds it in a clockwise direction. Then she and her horse head for the top point of the triangle, which they circle in a clockwise direction. Once around the third and final barrel, the racer gallops at full-speed toward the finish line. When the horse hits the finish line, the clock stops. Riders are penalized if they knock over barrels. And after penalties are factored in, the rider with the lowest time wins. It's pure adrenaline!

ROCCO SAYS

Ideally, a horse will take only three strides while circling a barrel.

BULL RIDING

Whereas bareback riding requires unbelievable strength and saddle bronc riding requires a keen awareness of timing, bull riding is all about balance.

RODEO TRIVIA

In bull riding, you'll often hear cowboys refer to a bull as "rank." This term is reserved for only the best of the best bucking stock, including horses, and it signifies an animal that bucks better than the rest. Bull riders live to ride "rank" bulls, because doing so provides riders with the greatest chance of earning a high score and an even higher paycheck.

In this event, the bull is led into the chute, where the rider attaches his rigging, in this case a "bull rope," to the bull. A bull rope is a braided length of cotton rope that circles the bull's chest, just behind its forelegs. The rider eases onto the bull and slips his gloved hand into a splice in the bull rope that serves as a handle. He then slides his inner thighs up as close to the bull rope as possible and places his spurs in

front of the bull rope. The rider then nods for the gate to be opened, and the wild ride begins.

HOW TO RIDE A MECHANICAL BULL

First, straddle the bull, then place your right hand palm up underneath the bull rope. (If you're left-handed, perform the opposite of all we describe.) Scoot your bottom and legs as close to your hand and the bull rope as possible. Then place your boots in front of the bull rope. Raise your left hand in the air as if pointing toward the sky. Nod to the mechanical bull operator when you're ready to ride.

Here are some pointers for when the bull starts moving:

- Hold on tight.
- Squeeze the bull's torso with your legs and heels.
- Remain as close to vertical as possible throughout the ride.
- If the bull moves to the right, throw your left arm back and to the left.
- If the bull moves to the left, throw your left arm forward and to the right.
- If the bull raises its head, allow your body to bend forward at the waist.
- If the bull raises its hind end, raise your rear-end off the bull's back as if attempting to stand up.

Do these things and you'll be that much closer to staying on the bull for the full eight seconds.

The rider's goal is to remain on the bull for the full eight seconds without allowing his free hand, which ideally is held high above his head for balance, to touch any part of the animal, which would result in a disqualification. The rider can earn bonus points for spurring the bull, which means lifting his outside leg away and toward the bull's torso as the bull is bucking. At the end of the eight seconds, a horn blows and the rider comes off the bull.

RODEO TRIVIA
It's a tenet of bull riding that the most dangerous part of the event is not the actual riding of the bull. The majority of injuries and accidents occur while the rider is lowering himself into the chute to get on the bull and when he's trying to get off the bull after completion of the ride—that is, if the bull lets him stick around that long.

And that's that. The perf is over.

However, that's not the end of the story. What happens behind the scenes, both to make all of the above possible and as a result of the above, is a whole different story.

INJURIES

When it comes to rodeo, injuries such as broken backs, arms, legs, ankles, and hands; punctured lungs; torn rotator cuffs; ruptured knee ligaments; severed fingers; crushed tailbones; and concussions are almost as common as the sunrise.

RODEO TRIVIA
There's one thing all rodeos cowboys agree with: It's not a matter of *if* you're going to get hurt; it's a matter of *when*.

To almost all other athletes, injuries of this nature would mean, at one end of the spectrum, being sidelined and, at the other, retirement. But to the bull, saddle bronc, and bareback rider, to the barrel racer, steer wrestler, and tie-down and team ropers, injuries like these are perceived as nothing more than scratches that must be patched up and padded, all before the next rodeo or, more often, the next event. There's a reason why this is the norm rather than the exception in rodeo.

Rodeo is not like other sports, where athletes are placed on injured reserve and sit on the sideline collecting a paycheck for weeks on end or even an entire season. There's no such luxury in rodeo. If the cowboy doesn't play hurt, he doesn't collect a paycheck. And if he doesn't collect a paycheck, he can't afford to travel or pay his entry fee to participate in another rodeo—and he soon finds himself off the road and trying to find work that will help pay for a Mt. Everest of medical bills.

When a cowboy gets hurt, the medical expenses come out of his own pocket. Why? Because no insurance company will insure him because of the risks inherent in their chosen sport. So, for a tough injury like a shattered ankle, it may mean the cowboy has to spend the rest of the season—or longer—paying off his bills. However, this is a part of the sport that rodeo cowboys full accept.

As with every other part of cowboy life, family—whether of the blood or extended variety—often jumps in to lend a helping hand. Through fund-raisers or benefit rodeos, the cowboy community will rally around one of its own to make sure that person is well cared for and able to continue the cowboy lifestyle.

But the rodeo community doesn't look out only for its own. Nope, they play an integral role in many charitable organizations. For example, at nearly every rodeo these days, one night will be deemed Tough Enough to Wear Pink Night, in which cowboys in the arena and in the stands wear pink in solidarity with and to raise money for the fight against breast cancer. There's also the Justin Crisis Fund, which aids rodeo cowboys who don't recover from their injuries, and many other nonprofit organizations set up to provide aid where aid is needed.

Another facet of rodeo life that cowboys not only have to

contend with but overcome is the rigor of traveling to and from rodeos.

ON THE ROAD

When you think of a college football team traveling cross country, most likely they board a chartered jet to escort them to their destination and back. But the same is not true for rodeo cowboys. Only the elite rodeo cowboys enjoy such as luxury. For any event that requires a horse, the rodeo cowboy has to trailer the horse to wherever he is headed. And when you consider that he may have a performance in Houston, Texas, on Saturday night and have to be in Pendleton, Oregon, by Monday morning for a slack competition, things can get a bit tricky.

For that reason, many cowboys travel as a group—to trade off driving, to keep costs low, and for company. Roughstock riders may be the exception, for they are able to travel light, as their equipment is minimal, which affords them the luxury of traveling by plane to many of their rodeo destinations—that is, if they can financially afford to do so.

Masterminding a rodeo travel schedule can often spell the difference between having money—sometimes millions of dollars—in your pocket at the end of the season and being in debt going into the start of a new season in January. This is where a business mind trumps athletic ability any day of the week. As with ranching, it is the rodeo cowboy who knows how to make the most of every penny who finds himself with the best balance sheet at the end of the season. It is the combination of athleticism and business savvy that will lead the fortunate cowboy to the most-sought after perf in rodeo—the National Finals Rodeo.

High-level collegiate rodeo cowboys aim to finish their season competing at what they affectionately call the "Pizza Hut on the Hill." For the rest of us, that's the Collegiate National Finals Rodeo, or CNFR, set in Casper, Wyoming. The CNFR earned this moniker because the arena where the event takes place sits in close proximity to this pizza chain, which resides at an elevation overlooking the rest of town and can be seen from miles away.

THE NATIONAL FINALS RODEO

Only the season's top fifteen money-earners in each event qualify for the NFR. This means that less than a minute fraction of card-carrying PRCA rodeo cowboys earn the right to attend this event.

The NFR is no run-of-the-mill rodeo. Some 175,000 spectators attend the event over its ten-day duration, where $5.5 million in prize money is at stake.

Furthermore, the NFR is the one rodeo of the year where the rodeo cowboys get to choose the stock they ride, rope, and wrestle. If you think for one second the cowboys pick second-rate animals, guess again. There's no way a cowboy could live with himself is he chose less than the best to compete against. This means that the toughest bucking horses and bulls and the fastest and strongest calves and steers are selected to battle the cowboys. It's the only way to prove who really is the best.

But the rodeo cowboy's role in the selection process does not stop there. He also gets to choose the pickup men and bullfighters. The pickup men retrieve saddle bronc and bareback riders from their horses—while the horses are running wild and still bucking. They also ensure that horses, bulls, steers, and calves exit the arena without injuring themselves or any cowboy or rodeo personnel. The bullfighters have a more focused role. They place themselves in harm's way to make sure neither the rodeo cowboy nor any contract personnel are injured by the bulls. We could devote an entire chapter to these unsung heroes of the rodeo, but these are some of the most obvious in a long list of responsibilities managed by pickup men and bullfighters. They are also some of the most talented athletes you'll see at the NFR, or pretty much any other rodeo for that matter, and they're not even competing in the perf. Rather, they are in place to make sure everyone in the arena is safe. Because of their immeasurable value, NFR cowboys choose only the very best pickup men and bullfighters to keep an eye on them when they are doing what they do.

The organization of NFR perfs is unique. Every cowboy competes in each of the go-rounds that take place over the course of the ten-night affair. Each round has a go-round winner. At the end of the ten days, an aggregate winner is also crowned. The aggregate winner is the rodeo cowboy with the highest combined scores in the roughstock events or the lowest times in the timed events over the entire ten days. When all monies earned over the course of a season are combined with the total purse earned at the NFR, the cowboy with the highest dollar amount won is crowned World Champion in his chosen event. But that's not all. The cowboy who has earned the most prize money among all rodeo cowboys in all events combined (regular season and NFR earnings) wins the most sought-after title in all of rodeo: All-Around Cowboy. There's one winner every year, and only a handful of cowboys have won it more than once.

Ready to retire and hit the rodeo circuit? We didn't think so, and neither are we. But for those of us who can't hit the conventional rodeo circuit, there is another type of rodeo that's aimed at the working cowboy.

RANCH RODEO

Ranch rodeo is governed by the Working Ranch Cowboy Association. Now, you don't qualify for ranch rodeo simply by winning a certain amount of money in sanctioned events. Nope, something more is needed. The rules require a competitor to be a real-deal working ranch cowboy who has been employed in a working cow-calf operation for a designated number of months. For the majority of ranch rodeo cowboys, this is no problem. In fact, it's an almost laughable requirement, as most, if not all, have worked, and continue to work each and every day of their lives, in the field. Because of this, and because of the events involved in it, ranch rodeo is more like the original rodeos that took place more than a century and a half ago than is conventional rodeo. We're not saying it's better or worse, just different.

ROCCO SAYS
The cattle used in ranch rodeo are wilder and less accustomed to being handled than those used in conventional rodeo. Cowboys refer to them as "fresh cattle."

There is one significant thing that distinguishes ranch from conventional rodeo. With the exception of team roping, conventional rodeo is an individual event. Ranch rodeo is wholly a team event, composed of cowboys from a given ranch. The idea is to mirror working ranch life as closely as possible in the competitive arena, thereby preserving the historical roots of the sport. It's up to the teams to decide who performs what in each event.

BRONC RIDING

The first event is bronc riding. It's roughly the same as saddle bronc riding in what we've termed conventional rodeo. However, there are two main differences. First, the rider uses a standard working saddle rather than the modified saddle used in saddle bronc. Second, where the saddle bronc rider is allowed to hold on to the rein with only one hand and the free hand cannot touch the horse without disqualification, a different rule applies in ranch rodeo. It's simply "ride as ride can." That means that, just like when cowboys were

breaking broncs at the ranch or on the range, the rider uses one hand on a rein and the other on whatever will keep him on the horse's back. That is, he can hold the saddle horn, the horse's mane, or the horse's neck or hind end—anything for balance. As with saddle bronc, the cowboy must ride for eight seconds, and is judged upon the same criteria as his counterpart in the conventional rodeo.

Sam Dove

MUGGING

The next event is called mugging. This event has its roots in cowboys on the range needing to be able to restrain a cow so that it can be doctored when injured or ill. Here's how it works: One cowboy, who is mounted on a horse, ropes a yearling (i.e., a one-year-old cow) and guides it to a designated area, where three other cowboys flank it or maneuver it onto its side, and then tie three of the cow's legs together. When all three legs are tied, the clock stops and the team with the lowest time wins.

REAL-DEAL PROFILE

When you travel across the cattle country of the West, where cowboys abound, there are a handful of cowboys who stand out from the rest. One such man is Sam Dove, foreman of the CF Ranch in Alpine, Texas.

Sam earned his reputation the hard way: by putting his intentions to work. He has done this not only wherever he has labored as a hand, but he's also in the competitive arena as a participant in authentic-as-it-gets ranch rodeo.

Although Sam has won or placed high in this back-to-roots rodeo, and has the belt buckles to show for it, he knows that his competitive endeavors would mean nothing if it weren't for the history that makes such events possible. And there's no question in anyone's mind that Sam would give up his rodeo achievements in a heartbeat if it guaranteed him just one more minute on the open range, living the life he loves.

CATTLE SORTING

Cattle sorting, which is much the same as cutting cattle on the ranch, is next. In this event, a herd of cows with numbers on their backs are placed at one end of the arena. The announcer calls out a number. One cowboy locates the cow with that number and cuts it from the herd. Once the cow is cut, three of the cowboy's teammates, who are also on horseback, use their horsemanship to keep the herd separated from the cut cow. The announcer continues to call out numbers and the process is repeated for a designated period of time. The team that cuts the most cows from the herd in the allotted time, and keeps them separated, wins the event.

TEAM BRANDING

As with the other events, the next one also has its roots in ranching. It's called team branding, and it's essentially the same activity that takes place on a ranch. Here, a cowboy on horseback ropes the hind legs of a calf and leads it to two of his teammates, who flank the calf and remove the rope. The fourth teammate then "brands" the calf with a branding iron coated with a powder, such as lime, and places the branding iron back in the bucket containing the powder, at which point the clock is stopped. The team completing the branding in the fastest time wins.

WILD COW MILKING

We've now arrived at one of the wildest—and often most entertaining—events in ranch rodeo. It's an event where there's no question that the cow has the upper hand, and there's very little the cowboys can do to change that. It's called wild cow milking, and it's exactly what it sounds like. In this event, one cowboy ropes a cow—and we're not talking some five-hundred-pound yearling. We're talking a thousand-pound-plus animal that can be as stubborn as they come. One cowboy, mounted on a horse, ropes the cow and brings her across a starting line, where his teammates are waiting. At this point, they have the almost insurmountable task of getting the cow under control, which is the last thing the cow wants, and squeezing some milk from its udders into a container. (The mounted cowboy can dismount and help his teammates, if necessary.) Once the milk is obtained, one of the cowboys sprints with the container of milk to a designated area and hands it to a judge. There must be enough milk in the bottle so that when the judge tips it over, milk spills to the ground. If milk pours out, the team with the fastest time wins.

RODEO TRIVIA

Wild cow milking is not just not for laughs. It, too, has its roots in ranching. There are many situations on a ranch where a cowboy needs to obtain milk from a cow. For example, a momma cow may have an infected teat, and her baby might not be able to nurse, so the cowboys have to obtain the milk from another cow so that they can feed the baby cow.

And that's ranch rodeo for you.

Rodeo of either variety is as much a part of cowboy life as any other. Not only does it allow the cowboy to carry on traditions that date back to the cowboy's origin, but it provides them with an arena in which to better themselves in a way they love. When you get the chance, go out and watch a rodeo, or at least tune into one on your television. It will provide you with a look into cowboy history and will allow you to see some top-notch athletes show off their skills. Who knows, you might just get urge to hop on a bull or run a few barrels. If you do, get some qualified instruction and go for it! It will be one thrill you'll never forget. Just don't make it memorable because you land yourself in the emergency room.

INTO THE SUNSET
The Essence of the Great American Cowboy

Like everything the cowboy does, keeping it simple is key—and that's what we're going to do here.

With that philosophy in mind, it all comes down to this:

Being a cowboy isn't about roping calves, riding bulls, or polishing off a fifth of Jim Beam. Being a cowboy is a mind-set that permeates everything the cowboy is and does. It is a mental toughness that sees in every hardship a challenge to overcome the impossible, and it is having a presence that demands the highest level of respect and that offers even more respect in return. It is about knowing when to be self-reliant and when to team up with others to battle the situation at hand. It is about caring for the land, animals, and the people you love, and it is about leaving the world better off than how you found it. That's what being a cowboy is all about.

We hope this book has imparted to you a great deal of knowledge about the life and times of the Great American Cowboy and has instilled in each and every one of you a deep respect and profound appreciation for this oh-so-American institution that both of us know and feel within our hearts. Even more, we hope that you can, and will, incorporate what you've learned into as many aspects of your life as possible.

And if you take only one bit of information away from the time you've spent with us, we hope it is this: The most important characteristics defining a cowboy are those that can't be seen with the eye; they can only be felt in the heart and soul of everyone with whom the cowboy comes in contact.

Now go out and make us proud.

Be a cowboy.

How to Live Like a Cowboy If You Can't Actually Become One

A RESOURCE AND REFERENCE GUIDE FOR THE URBAN COWBOY

Not all of us are cut out for the cowboy life, and even among those who are, few are fortunate enough to be able to live that simple life out on the open range each and every day. But that doesn't mean we can't savor the cowboy way of life no matter where we are. Here are some suggestions for where to go, what to buy, and much, much more:

THE ULTIMATE WORKING RANCH COWBOY SCHOOL
Arizona Cowboy College
Scottsdale, Arizona
www.cowboycollege.com

ALL THINGS COWBOY: SHOOTING, RIDING, WORKING CATTLE, AND MORE
M Lazy C Ranch
Lake George, Colorado
www.mlazyc.com

COWBOY SHOOTING SCHOOL
Annie-Bianco Ellett
Cave Creek, Arizona
www.outlawannie.com

DANCE INSTRUCTION
D.G. Dance
Dennis Giullian
Denver, Colorado
www.grizzlyrose.com (click on "Dance Lessons")

RODEO SCHOOLS
Gary Leffew Bull Riding Schools
www.leffewbullridingworld.com

Joe Beaver Roping Schools
www.joebeaver.com

APPAREL MEGA STORES
Boot Barn Live West
www.bootbarn.com

Sheplers
www.sheplers.com

COWBOY HATS
J. W. Brooks Custom Hat Co.
www.jwbrookscustomhats.com

DRESS SHIRTS
Rockmount Ranch Wear
www.rockmount.com

COWBOY BELTS, WALLETS, AND OTHER LEATHER GOODS
Leatherworks
Pat Brantley
1002 Arthur St.
Burkburnett, Texas 76354
(940) 569-0555

BELT BUCKLES
Montana Silversmiths
www.montanasilversmiths.com

JEANS
Cinch
www.cinchjeans.com

Levi's
www.levi.com

Wrangler
www.wrangler.com

BOOTMAKERS
Justin Boots
www.justinboots.com

Ariat
www.ariat.com

SPURS
George Blackwood Spurs
www.blackwoodspurs.com

J.M. Capriola Co. and Garcia Bit and Spur Co.
www.capriolas.com

HORSE SUPPLY AND TACK
Bent H Ranch Products
www.horsemassagers.com

CSI Saddlepads
www.csipads.com

Dynamite Horseman Supply
www.dynamitehorsemansupply.com

Mikmar Bit Company
www.mikmar.com

ROPES
Cactus Ropes
www.cactusropes.com

Classic Ropes
Equibrand
www.equibrand.com

ROPING DUMMIES AND AIDS
Heel-O-Matic Training Systems
www.heelomatic.com

The Jakesteer
Rope-O-Matic
www.rope-o-matic.com/jakesteer

Sparky Jr.
Rocking K
www.rockingkarena.com/sparkyjr

MUSICAL INSTRUMENTS
Guitars
C.F. Martin and Co.
www.martinguitar.com

Harmonicas
Hohner, Inc.
www.hohnerusa.com

DUTCH OVENS AND COOKING SUPPLY
Cajun Cast Iron
www.cajuncastiron.com

FIREARMS
Sturm, Ruger & Co.
www.ruger-firearms.com

Winchester Repeating Arms
www.winchesterguns.com

MUSICIANS AND POETS
Don Edwards
www.donedwardsmusic.com

Jerry Jeff Walker
www.jerryjeff.com

Pat James
www.patjames.net

Red Steagall
www.redsteagall.com

Robert Earl Keen
www.robertearlkeen.com

R.W. Hampton
www.rwhampton.com

Sons of the San Joaquin
www.thesons.com

Tex Ritter

www.b-westerns.com/ritter.htm

Waddie Mitchell
www.waddiemitchell.com

COWBOY AND WESTERN PHOTOGRAPHY AND ART
AZPhotos.net

John Beckett
Beckett & Beckett Photography
www.jbeckettphoto.com

Carrie Brantley
www.brantleyphotoworks.com

Charles E. Brooks
Brooks Photography
www.brooksphotog.com

Kevin Kibsey
Villas & Verandahs Fine Art Gallery
www.villasandverandas.com/kk.htm

MAGAZINES
American Cowboy
www.americancowboy.com

Cowboys & Indians
www.cowboysindians.com

Western Horseman
www.westernhorseman.com

TELEVISION
Country Music Television
www.cmt.com

RFD-TV
www.rfdtv.com

HONKY-TONKS AND SALOONS TO VISIT
Billy Bob's Texas
Fort Worth, Texas
www.billybobstexas.com

Buckhorn Bar
Laramie, Wyoming
www.buckhornbar.com

Buffalo Chip Saloon
Cave Creek, Arizona
www.buffalochipsaloon.com

Greasewood Flat
Scottsdale, Arizona
www.greasewoodflat.net

The Grizzly Rose
Denver, Colorado
www.grizzlyrose.com

The Mint Bar
Sheridan, Wyoming
(307) 674-9696

PLACES TO GO AND THINGS TO SEE

Cheyenne Frontier Days
Cheyenne, Wyoming
www.cfdrodeo.com

Fort Worth Stockyards National Historic District
Fort Worth, Texas
www.fortworthstockyards.org

Lincoln County Cowboy Symposium
Ruidoso Downs, New Mexico
www.cowboysymposium.org

National Cowboy and Western Heritage Museum
Oklahoma City, Oklahoma
www.nationalcowboymuseum.org

National Cowboy Poetry Gathering
Western Folklife Center
Elko, Nevada
www.westernfolklife.org

National Western Stock Show
Denver, Colorado
www.nationalwestern.com

Pacific Livestock Auction
Chandler, Arizona
www.pacificlivestockauction.com

ProRodeo Hall of Fame and Museum of the American
Cowboy
Colorado Springs, Colorado
www.prorodeohalloffame.com

Texas Cowboy Poetry Gathering
Alpine, Texas
www.cowboy-poetry.org

Working Ranch Cowboys Association World Championship
Ranch Rodeo
Amarillo, Texas
www.wrca.org

Wrangler National Finals Rodeo
Las Vegas, NV
www.nfrexperience.com

ORGANIZATIONS

American Chuckwagon Association
www.chuckwagon.org

American Paint Horse Association
www.apha.com

American Quarter Horse Association
www.aqha.com

Appaloosa Horse Club
www.appaloosa.com

Cowboy Mounted Shooting Association
www.cowboymountedshooting.com

Professional Bull Riders
www.pbrnow.com

Professional Rodeo Cowboys Association
www.prorodeo.com

United States Border Collie Club
www.bordercollie.org

Women's Professional Rodeo Association
www.wpra.com

A Taste of Cowboy Vocabulary

Barn sour: Describes a horse that is uncomfortable being alone

Broke: Describes a horse that is trained

Bull: An adult male cow

Bull-calf: A young male cow that has not been castrated

Calf: A young cow

Cantle: The rear upward-sloping part of a saddle

Colt: A male foal up to two years in age

Dam: The female parent of a foal

Filly: A female foal up to two years in age

Floating: The act by a horse of grinding its food to chew it, which provides for better nutritional utilization of the food

Foal: A baby horse

Gelding: A male horse that has been castrated

Hackamore: A bridle without a bit

Hand: Unit of measurement used to assess the height of a horse (one hand equals four inches)

Hazer: The cowboy to the right of the steer in steer wrestling

Heifer: A female cow up to two years old or up to the time she gives birth to a calf

Hobbles: Straps attached to a horse's front legs to prevent it from wandering off

Horse-length: Eight feet

Lame: Describes a horse with the medical condition laminitis, an inflammation of the laminae (tissue in the hoof), which causes the horse to limp

Lope: A three-beated gait

Mare: A female horse

Maverick: An unbranded cow

Outlaw: A horse that likely will never be broke

Perf: Short for performance, as used in rodeos

Pommel: The front of a saddle

Rodeo: A sport event; a verb used to designate a cowboy's participation in that event (as in: "He rodeos up in Casper this weekend.")

Sacking out: Desensitizing a horse as a part of saddle training

Sire: The male parent of a foal

Sored up: An adjective used by rodeos cowboys to describe a feeling of being beaten-up from competing (as in: "I am all sored up after getting bucked from that bronc.")

Sound: An adjective used to describe a horse that is not lame

Steer: A male cow that has been castrated

Stirrup: The part of a saddle in which the rider places his foot

Tapadero: Leather cover that protects the foot while it is in the stirrup

Tree: The wooden core of a saddle

Weanling: A weaned foal

West Texas rain: Dust

COWBOY LINGO FOR A HORSE

Bronc

Broomtail

Cayuse

Fantail

Gut-twister
Hammerhead
Hay-burner
Killer
Nag
Plug
Sunfishing son of a gun

HORSE COLORS
Appaloosa
Bay
Black
Blue roan
Brown
Buckskin
Chestnut
Cremello
Dapple gray
Dun
Flea-bitten gray
Gray
Grulla
Line-back dun
Liver chestnut
Overo
Palomino
Pinto
Roan
Sorrel
Sabino
Tobiano
Tovero
White or albino
Zebra dun

FACIAL MARKINGS ON A HORSE

Bald Face

Blaze

Bonnet

Snip

Star

Star and Stripe

Star, Stripe and Snip

Stripe

Acknowledgments

John Beckett, Annie Bianco-Ellett, Pat Brantley, Lloyd Bridwell, Lori Bridwell, Charlie Brooks, J.W. Brooks, TaNaye Carroll, Craig Carter, David Charles, Gwendolyn Colby, Betty Dove, Sam Dove, Dennis Giullian, The Grizzly Rose, Ed Hanks, Stacy Hashimoto, Natelle Huntzinger, RuthAnn Huntzinger, Kevin Kibsey, Adam Korn, Brad McCaskill, the Mercer Rodeo Company, Brenda Myers, Randy Myers, Elaine Pawlowski, Brandy Pellegrini, Gerry Pellegrini, Papa Joe Samsill, Pattie Simoes, Damian Wachman, George Walsh, David Wechter, our families and friends, and the countless cattle dogs, horses, cows, and cowboys who compose the landscape of the American West.

A special thank-you to:

Carrie Brantley, personal editor, photographer, Texan, and, most of all, friend;

Charlie Brooks, whose exceptional work ethic would make him a "good hand" on any spread in the American West;

Sorche Fairbank, who believed in this project from day one and guided us like a seasoned ranch boss throughout our literary journey;

Dick Huntzinger, a cowboy's kind of cowboy and a third pair of eyes we would have been hard-pressed to have lived without;

Amy Bendell, whose passion for and expertise in bringing this book to life is a testament to cowboys everywhere; and

Kevin Kibsey, a modern-day Frederic Remington if ever there was one.

ABOUT THE AUTHORS

ROCCO WACHMAN is the host of six seasons of Country Music Television's hit series *Cowboy U* and is the senior instructor at the Arizona Cowboy College. He lives in Scottsdale, Arizona.

www.cowboycollege.com

MATT PELLEGRINI is a cowboy enthusiast, chuck wagon cooking aficionado, writer, and attorney who spent more than two years working among cowboys and researching this book. He lives in Denver, Colorado.

www.mattpellegrini.com